atlantic seafood

atlantic seafood

recipes from Chef Michael Howell

NIMBUS
PUBLISHING
NIMBUS.CA

Nimbus Publishing Limited
PO Box 9166, Halifax, NS , B3K 5M8
(902) 455-4286
www.nimbus.ca

Printed and bound in Canada
NB1524
Design by Jesse Marchand
Author photo by Shannon George
Cover image and interior images (excluding pages 24, 36, 42, 49, 66, 78, 101, 114, 118 & 126)
    by Colleen Dagnall and Bob Federer,
    Shooterbug Photography—www.shooterbug.com

Library and Archives Canada Cataloguing in Publication

Title: Atlantic seafood / recipes from Chef Michael Howell.
Names: Howell, Michael, 1962- author.
Identifiers: Canadiana 20200160133 | ISBN 9781771088954 (softcover)
Subjects: LCSH: Cooking (Seafood) | LCGFT: Cookbooks.
Classification: LCC TX747 .H73 2021 | DDC 641.6/92—dc23

Nimbus Publishing acknowledges the financial support for its publishing activities from the Government of Canada, the Canada Council for the Arts, and from the Province of Nova Scotia. We are pleased to work in partnership with the Province of Nova Scotia to develop and promote our creative industries for the benefit of all Nova Scotians.

Foreword

It is hard to believe that ten years have passed since this book was first published. Yes, it's a cookbook—but it's also partly my autobiography.

Much has changed since 2010. I sold Tempest, my restaurant, and while I am still cooking at the Green Turtle Club in Abaco, Bahamas, and at many special events, my life has shifted with the growth and success of Devour! The Food Film Fest, which I created as I wrote this book, and which has now taken on a life of its own as my life's purpose. I curate food films and events around the world and bring chefs and filmmakers together to be inspired by one another.

But I continue to celebrate this book's timely capture of my ethos from ten years ago. Cooking sustainably and from the heart is still the essence of what I continue to promote. Seafood stocks are dwindling globally, more and more species are at risk, and the oceans are in danger of depletion beyond repair. Chefs like Robert Clark and Ned Bell, and organizations like Slow Food, the World Food Programme, World Central Kitchen, the Environmental Defense Fund, and the Ecology Action Centre advocate tirelessly on behalf of species that cannot speak for themselves. Please think wisely, and try to purchase locally whenever possible.

I thanked many suppliers at the beginning of the original edition. Today I want to thank you, the reader, for bringing the second publication of this book to life. Books are disappearing, so to see renewed interest in one is a joy.

I would like to repeat my thanks to my mentor, Chef Joho, who continues to be a part of my culinary and professional life, and to my current employers, Adam and Sarah Ann at the Green Turtle Club, who have stuck with me as I've come and gone for twenty years (and who want me to write a Green Turtle Club cookbook!). Also to my wife, Mary, and my children, Burton and Olivia, thank you for your continued support through thick and thin.

Eat more fish!

Table of Contents

Introduction

The sea is in my blood. Some might scoff when a person has the audacity to aver he has oceanic lineage—they would expect a raft of hyperbole and icebergs of irreverent anecdotes from that claimant. But I truly am one of those whose lineage can be traced through to those who went to sea in ships.

My grandfather, Captain Jack Howell, was from Grand Manan, New Brunswick. Captain Jack was a successful fisherman, and during Prohibition he allegedly supplemented his income as a rum-runner on his boat, the *Barbara J. Howell.*

The *Barbara J. Howell*

My grandmother, Mary O'Brien, was from Gloucester, Massachusetts, and apparently Captain Jack met her while ashore after a "working" trip through coastal US waters; they married and my father, John Joseph Howell, was born shortly thereafter. Alas, the Bureau of Alcohol, Tobacco, and Firearms caught up with Captain Jack, convicted him of rum-running, and sent him to the Long Island Penitentiary for eighteen months. After his

release, Captain Jack and his new family moved to Hebron, Nova Scotia.

John naturally followed in his father's footsteps as a fisherman and travelled between Canada and the US chasing the fish, first as a mate and then later as a captain. After a first marriage and subsequent divorce in the US, he returned to Canada in 1961 and married Diane Burton. Shortly thereafter I was born to them in Yarmouth, Nova Scotia, in 1962.

My father led a short but full life. Mostly he was at sea, away from my mother for two to three weeks at a time. He would return home for a couple of days after each trip to spend frivolously, live large, and party hard with a fistful of newly earned cash. Then he would kiss my mother goodbye and return immediately to the seas in the endlessly repetitive cycle that is the life of a fisherman. At the tender age of thirty-six (when I was only four), he fell overboard on one such fishing trip and drowned in New Brunswick's Bay of Chaleur. Poignantly enough, on this particular herring fishing journey he was not the captain but was working as the cook.

To put the past behind, my now-single mother moved to Chester with me, my younger brother, Burton, and infant sister, Michele. Chester is a tranquil seaside resort town an hour from Halifax, well-known for sailing and the spectacular retreats of wealthy Americans on "The Peninsula." When I was eleven, my mother married our neighbour John Misick, a Bermudian-born, UK-educated, Dalhousie University business professor, and thus my life changed irrevocably. Had John Howell not perished, it is most likely that today I would be a fisherman.

I finished high school, attended Dalhousie University in Halifax, and for my early adult years I was a professional actor and director based in Toronto. Of course, the irony of it all is that most young actors supplement their living by working in restaurants, and I was no different, working as a waiter in five different restaurants over the course of eight years, in between various acting and directing jobs and a good stint at the Shaw Festival in the mid-1980s.

When I married my wife, Mary, in 1992 and her stage management job took us to Chicago, I decided to redirect my energies into becoming a chef—I had long enjoyed throwing big dinner parties and I was familiar with the restaurant world already. So in 1994 I started at the Cooking and Hospitality Institute of Chicago, and graduated fourteen months later.

My first job after school was at a venerated French restaurant in Chicago called The Everest Room under my mentor, Chef Jean Joho. After only three months as a commis, or junior cook, I was promoted to poissonier, or fish chef. I spent almost two years there, learning French technique and polish in an über-sophisticated restaurant well regarded across America.

Subsequent jobs took me initially to Detroit and then back to the seacoast—first to Newburyport, Massachusetts (near Boston), then on to New York City to work at a well regarded Italian restaurant on Staten Island, Carol's Cafe. Finally though, after most of a year in New York and closing in on ten years running around North America, we finally burned out on city life. Mary was six months pregnant with our second child when I found a wonderful job as the executive chef at the Green Turtle Club in Abaco, Bahamas. This small island, with a population of three hundred, was the complete antithesis of the life we had hitherto led.

In the kitchen of the hotel, all manners of seafood crossed my stoves as I expanded my repertoire. The island inhabitants grew to be very dear to us and we rode through four hurricanes with them between 1999 and 2002. It was an idyllic period to work in this tropical paradise and watch our very young children grow into little beauties.

But after three years we were ready for our own business and to make our own decisions. We returned to civilization, with sadness for having to leaving the tranquil island life behind, but also excitement at the prospect of finally being our own bosses.

When the opportunity arose back in Canada to purchase the restaurant that was to become Tempest, I persuaded my wife and children that returning home for me was a great opportunity for us all. With my history as a native Nova Scotian and my lineage as the son of a fisherman, we stood a good chance of carving out a successful niche for ourselves. The Annapolis Valley would be a wonderful place to raise our kids and open a restaurant. Being restaurateurs in a fledgling wine area also sounded attractive to us.

While we cook many things at Tempest (being as we are in the heart of a rich agricultural region) we focus on seafood. Both tourists and locals alike revel in the flavours of fresh seafood well presented. And when we can source the most succulent morsels from the land and sea, we can transport you to the ocean's shore.

This is a thread that binds all of my cooking—that a well-prepared meal can convey you to a place you cherish in memory, or inspire you to dream of a place you would like to go. When you savour a well-made bouillabaisse, you instinctually think of the south of

France and the beaches of the Côte d'Azure. Flavours and aromas can evoke these strong memories or can provide solace for those bound by circumstance and unable to travel.

One of my favourite seafood memories harks back to 1986, when I spent a summer sailing the coasts of France and Spain with my cousin Michael D. The day we picked up our boat in Sete and departed on our six-week cruise, we spent the morning swimming and snorkelling off the beautiful harbour's breakwater. We discovered a cache of mussels in about six feet of water, harvested about two kilos of them, and took them back to the boat. I cooked them with some fresh linguini, a local white wine, a little cream, some garlic, and a couple nuggets of fresh French chevre. With the sun setting in the west, we revelled in this meal that we had harvested and prepared ourselves, and dreamed of the adventure to come. I remember that evening today as clearly as if it were last night.

I hope that the recipes in this book will take you to a place that you either want to visit or remember fondly. The Maritimes and New England still offer some of the most enchanting scenery in the world. The bounty of the sea is available most everywhere and with a little diligence, you too can create a meal that will take you to the wharf, beach, or boat that resides in your dreams.

Ethical Eating

In 2006 I traveled to Turin, Italy, for the first time to attend Terra Madre, a world gathering of food communities and influencers. Terra Madre is the biennial gathering of the global Slow Food movement, a one hundred thousand–plus member organization centred on the belief that we need to consume and support food production that is **good, clean, and fair**, and that is produced ethically and with respect for Mother Earth. As the leader of Slow Food Nova Scotia and a conscientious procurer of foods for my business, I was one of thirty chefs from across Canada, and one of a thousand chefs from around the world, invited to participate in this international gathering to discuss issues of globalization and localization, and to learn how the restaurant industry might help make changes for the better by setting better examples.

Not surprisingly, seafood was front and centre at many of these meetings and there were heated discussions. I had the good fortune to meet and share many passionate and eye-opening conversations with Chef Robert Clark of Vancouver's C Restaurant. Robert has long been an advocate for serving only sustainable seafood on the plates of the world's restaurants, and has pushed for the hospitality industry to adopt the rules and guidelines for ethical eating set out by associations like Sea Choice (www.seachoice.org), an organization dedicated to providing information on sustainable seafood choices.

Shortly after my return from Italy, I was invited by Nova Scotia's Ecology Action Centre to sit on a panel with Taras Grescoe, author of *Bottom Feeder,* a book about the ethics of eating seafood. Taras's book advocates that we need to embrace a paradigm shift in what we eat from the sea. He urges us to eat fewer predatory species and more of those species found lower on the food chain, not only for the protection of those species but also because bottom feeders tend to have less mercury and parasitic infection and have higher concentrations of healthy fish oils.

With these catalytic meetings fresh in my mind, I decided my restaurant would serve only sustainable species as outlined by watchdogs Sea Choice or Oceanwise. At Tempest I served haddock, but only line-caught haddock. I served swordfish, but only harpooned Atlantic swordfish. Instead of open–pen-farmed Atlantic salmon, I substituted Arctic Char from closed-containment Oceanwise-approved farms like Sustainable Blue. I tried to source only locally caught or approved land-based farmed species whenever possible. I stopped serving salmon, and I have not eaten ocean-farmed Atlantic salmon to this day. I experimented with herring and mackerel in creating recipes for my restaurant and for this book that appealed to sophisticated palates. I did not serve shark, bluefin tuna, Chilean sea bass, or fish that were not known to exist in Maritime waters.

I hope that as you use this cookbook, you will make your own informed choices about what to eat and consider the health of the seas when choosing to eat seafood. In particular, I would encourage you to educate yourself about the methods employed in catching fish and shellfish that result in significant unwanted bycatch, such as pelagic longlining, dredging, and massive factory trawling. In the recipes that follow, I make suggestions for ethical options if there are questions as to the sustainability of a particular fish or seafood.

Where to Buy Seafood

First of all, buy local products whenever you can. A fish that has travelled halfway around the world to get to you has a lot of ethical baggage and a large carbon footprint, and cannot possibly be as fresh as one bought locally. Find out where day-boat fishers land their catches. Go to places like Sambro or Halls Harbour or Digby when boats are arriving. Don't be shy! Speak up and offer to pay cash for a fresh fish.

Secondly, buy from a reputable dealer or grower. In the days when I owned Tempest, I purchased much of my seafood from Fisherman's Market and Sustainable Blue, a Nova Scotia closed-containment land-based fish farming operation for which I eventually became corporate chef. These days I try to use Afishionado Fishmongers in Halifax as much as possible. Hooked, in Toronto, is a great source for ethically sourced fish in Canada's largest city. And many larger retailers are changing their procurement policies. Whole Foods has also adopted traceability and MSC certification for most of its products. And it's not just high-end retailers either: in 2016, Walmart reported in its Global Responsibility Report that in the US, 100 percent of its fresh and frozen, farmed and wild seafood is sourced in accordance with its sustainability policy.

No matter where you end up shopping, ask at the counter what is fresh and what is local. For Tempest I used to buy all my mussels and scallops from Indian Point Marine Farms in Indian Point, NS. I also would buy from Eric and Sandra Publicover's The Fish Store; before they set up at the farmers' markets in Lunenburg, Chester, and Wolfville, they brought fresh local product with their truck and trailer to various communities in Nova Scotia. Birch Street Seafoods from the Digby area delivers fish to your door and advertises specials on its Facebook page. Try to avoid the big grocery retailers for your purchases unless they are certifying their sources.

Look for Marine Stewardship Council (MSC) certification on products. Be sure to always ask the provenance of the fish you are buying. And instead of buying typical species, think outside the box. Try herring or mackerel. Hake is a delicious and very affordable substitute for haddock. Arctic char instead of salmon. Albacore tuna instead of bluefin. Avoid fish like tilapia and basa, which are now farmed globally in uncertified environments; there is often significant environmental degradation in the places where they are grown.

Please try to avoid buying Chilean sea bass, bluefin tuna and skate—they are critically endangered. Try Alaskan black cod/sablefish, Fogo Island cod or Pacific halibut instead.

Lastly, catch it yourself. There is nothing more satisfying than catching your own striped bass or trout, especially when you know it has been caught sustainably, one fish at a time.

The Basics of Cooking Seafood

There are countless references in many cookbooks about the cooking times for different types of fish. But these calculations don't hold much weight. Fish is cooked when it is done to your satisfaction. When cooked, it should flake easily but never fall apart. Delicate and thin fish filets like sole, plaice, and flounder are perhaps the exception as the filets can be quite thin.

Flaky fish cooks faster, often twice as fast as dense fish. A piece of pan-roasted haddock will be cooked through in 5 minutes whereas a piece of swordfish may take 8–10 minutes.

If cooking fish in a pan, use a good-quality fish flipper to turn it over; otherwise your flaky filet will fall apart.

Try not to overcook fish. A tiny bit of translucency in the middle of a piece of fish means that it will be moist and not dry. Remember that fish continues to cook after coming out of the pan or oven.

Don't undercook shellfish. Mussels that are not thoroughly cooked take on an unpleasant gooey texture. Lobster is the same, but don't boil or steam it for 15–18 minutes like the old-time cookbooks say either. For a simple steamed lobster (best cooked in clean ocean seawater with a little seaweed in the pot), steam or boil a 1 ¼ pounder (½ kg) for 10–12 minutes.

Raw Fish—Sushi pervades our society nowadays and I, like many people, relish it on occasion. The fish must be of the utmost freshness, from a known supplier, and be completely free of blemishes or blood. I always investigate the fish for parasites (possible in larger carnivorous fish) by holding a piece up to a bright light bulb and looking through it for parasites. Tropical reef fish—grouper, large snapper, etc.—are particularly prone to parasitic infection. While I prepare sushi regularly (mostly for my wife, who loves it), I am not a sushi chef so have not included any recipes.

Methods of Cooking Seafood

Pan-roast/fry—A filet or fish steak is cooked in oil or fat in a pan on the stovetop. The fish is sometimes floured, breaded, or coated to create a pleasant crust for the fish. I prefer to use extra virgin olive or grapeseed oil. Grapeseed oil has a higher smoke point than other oils, so items cooked in it can be seared at a higher temperature resulting in a richer, golden-brown crust. Pan-roasting refers to the cooking method where a fish filet, steak, or even a whole fish is started on the stovetop and then transferred to the oven to finish cooking.

Deep-fry—Well known to us all, deep-frying is easy and fast. It does, however, require a deep fryer (or large pot of oil) and works best if you have a thermometer. The ideal temperature for frying fish is 350°F (175°–180°C). Fish is usually completely coated in a batter of some kind before being dipped into the hot oil. While it is bubbling in the oil, the fish actually gets steamed inside the coating while the coating becomes fried and crunchy.

Poached—Poaching fish means immersing it in a liquid and cooking it over relatively low heat. A court-bouillon (a mixture of water, wine or lemon, and spices) was the traditional poaching liquid for salmon or sole in the past, but modern chefs are utilizing newer broths and liquids—from duck consommé to a confit-style treatment where the fish is completely immersed in oil and cooked at a low temperature. It is then removed from the fat, drained, and served. This is a lovely, luxurious way to cook fish.

Roasted—A simple method, also referred to as the dry heat method. For example, a marinated side of salmon can often be cooked this way. When baked in an oven, the fish should be placed on a roasting pan or cookie sheet that has been topped with parchment or wax paper to avoid having the fish stick to the pan.

Grilled—The easy way! Firm-fleshed fish like tuna, salmon, and swordfish benefit from being cooked over an open flame. They take on the smoky flavour of the grill in addition to any marinade they may have been subjected to. An open-flame barbecue on a beach is a fun way to cook swordfish kebabs, salmon steaks, or even lobster. Avoid flare-ups by cooking over low heat. On a gas barbecue, grill fish on the medium setting rather than high. Let the grill preheat, then coat both the grill and the fish with some vegetable oil spray to prevent sticking, and finally put the fish onto the grill. Don't move it too early! Make sure a crust and/or good grill marks have formed before attempting to turn the fish.

Seviche—This method of preparing fish originates in Latin America. Fish or shellfish is cut into bite-size pieces and immersed for approximately two hours in a citrus-based liquid. This method coagulates the proteins without using heat, in effect "cooking" the fish. This is a particularly refreshing method in the summertime, when a dish like Scallop, Mango, and Passion Fruit Seviche (page 88), can be prepared earlier in the day, scooped into a martini glass at dinnertime, and served alfresco with a refreshing Nova Scotian L'Acadie Blanc, Italian Pinot Grigio, or Argentinian Torrontes wine.

Cooking Terminology

Blanching and Shocking—This refers to partly cooking something very quickly. At a certain point, the cooking process is abruptly stopped (to either accentuate a colour—as in green beans—or because further cooking will continue later). In the case of blanching, the item is cooked in a very hot liquid (water, oil, broth, etc.), before being pulled out. To stop the cooking process, the ingredients are sometimes "shocked" in the cold water of an "ice bath"—a large bowl of ice and water (page 9).

Deglaze—A method where wine, water, or another liquid is added to a pan after an ingredient has been sautéed in it. This releases anything stuck to the bottom of the pan and imbues that flavour into what you are cooking.

Mire Poix—A generic term in cooking referring to equal amounts of peeled, chopped carrot, onion, and celery, often used to make soups, stocks, and sauces.

Sweat—To cook slowly over medium-low heat. This method is generally used with vegetables to release the water within. As you "sweat" onions and carrots, they become somewhat translucent. You do not want to overcook the vegetables to the point of them turning brown, or even worse, black and burnt, when sweating them.

Measurements

Included are both metric and imperial measurements. In actuality, 200 ml is slightly less than a cup—it's around ⅞—and 100 ml is slightly less than a half cup—it's around ⅜. For the purposes of clarity and ease of measurement, we have rounded those measurements to one cup and half a cup respectively. Likewise, other conversions have been rounded to the nearest metric or imperial measurement. The recipes will not be affected by the slight variance in measure.

Stocks

While it is a bit old-fashioned to use stocks for sauces, they do have their use in chowders and soups. Instead of water as the base for chowder, a stock intensifies the flavour without having to add oceans of salt to a dish. Fish chowder always tastes better when fish stock is used.

At a good fish store, you can probably find the fish bones that you will need. Ask a fishmonger for some "white fish frames." (A fish frame is the skeleton and head of a fish after the meat is cut away.) The best kinds are haddock, halibut, hake, sole, flounder, and plaice. Oily fish, such as trout or mackerel, do not make good stock, as their flavours are too strong. Salmon frames can be used to make a stock, but because salmon is a relatively fatty fish (good omega-3 fatty acids of course) the stock will have a strong flavour—you would probably only want to make it if you are going to use it in a salmon chowder.

Fish heads can lend a desirable intensity to a fish stock, but if you are a little squeamish, the bones alone will result in a good stock. You could also buy a whole fish and filet it yourself if you feel adventurous. There are many excellent videos online that demonstrate how to effectively filet a fish.

Fish Stock

Yield ⤸ about 16 cups (4 litres)

bouquet garni (see below)
5 lbs (2.25 kg) fish frames, broken or cut into
    manageable pieces
2 large onions, peeled and roughly chopped
4 stalks celery, cleaned and chopped
1 head fennel (anise), cleaned and chopped
1 large leek, chopped and washed thoroughly
2 cups (500 ml) white wine, optional
16 cups (4 litres) water

Bouquet Garni
12 sprigs fresh thyme
12 peppercorns
12 parsley sprigs
6 bay leaves

cheesecloth

Prepare the bouquet garni by tying up the herbs in some cheesecloth so they can be retrieved when the stock is cooked.

In a pot large enough to hold the bones, combine all the ingredients. The fish bones should be completely covered with liquid. Bring to a boil, then reduce heat to a simmer. With a ladle, skim off any scum that rises to the surface.

Simmer for 2 hours, stirring occasionally. Cool briefly, then strain into another large pot or bowl. Cool to room temperature (an ice bath is the best method) and use immediately. May be stored in the refrigerator for 48 hours or frozen for future use.

TECHNIQUE TIDBIT

Ice baths—When trying to cool liquids quickly so that they can be refrigerated, chefs create an "ice bath." This is simply a large metal bowl or container that has been half filled with ice and cold water. To cool cooked foods, immerse them in the ice and water mixture. To cool liquids, place them in a small bowl inside the large bowl of ice. The ice chills the metal bowls quickly and the heat is conducted out of the liquid that you are trying to cool. Stirring occasionally helps the liquid cool faster. NEVER put a boiling hot liquid in your refrigerator, as it will warm up the other food inside before the fridge can cool it down.

Lobster Stock

Yield ✑ about 16 cups (4 litres)

Lobster stock can be used to make lobster bisque, the Shrimp Americaine Sauce (page 44), and Lobster Corn Chowder (page 48).

3 live lobsters (1 ¼ lbs/567 g each)
1 tsp (5 ml) extra virgin olive oil
1 onion, roughly chopped
1 carrot, roughly chopped
4 stalks celery, roughly chopped
16 cups (4 litres) water
2 bay leaves
2 Tbsp (30 ml) tomato paste
1 bunch fresh thyme
2 Tbsp (30 ml) sherry
2 cups (½ litre) white wine, optional

Preheat the oven to 425°F (220°C). In a large pot, bring a sufficient quantity of water to a boil to be able to immerse the lobsters. Prepare an ice bath (page 9). Boil the lobsters in the water for 8–10 minutes, then remove them to the ice bath to cool them quickly and stop the cooking process.

Discard the cooking water and clean out the pot. Drain the lobsters, crack them open with a cleaver or heavy knife, and remove the meat from the lobster bodies. The meat can be chopped and reserved for another use.

Place the lobster bodies, shell pieces, legs, and tail bits on a sheet pan and roast them in the oven for 10 minutes to evaporate any moisture. Add the oil to the cleaned pot over medium heat. Return the bodies and shells to the pot, add the vegetables, and sauté for 5 minutes before adding the water and remaining ingredients. Bring to a boil, then reduce heat to medium and simmer for 1 ½ hours.

Strain and reserve the liquid, and cool. Discard the solids. Portion the liquid into 4-cup (1-litre) containers for easy use later, and place the sealed containers in the fridge or freezer. Stock stored in the refrigerator should be used within 48 hours.

Sauces

A simple, unadorned morsel of grilled fish or shellfish can be transcendent on its own, but many of us prefer to add a little something to seafood, for moisture and texture. As some fish is relatively lean, it can be perceived as dry if fully cooked. But the addition of a butter sauce, citrus vinaigrette, or salsa can lift a dish from the plebeian to the ethereal if well-matched to the seafood it is served with. Below, I list some of my favourite styles of sauces and present a couple of recipes to give you an idea of what is possible with a little creativity.

Citrus

The most well-known accompaniment to fish is fresh lemon. The citrus punch complements the light flavour of fish and shellfish. Drawn butter (melted and clarified butter) with lemon is what we all imagine to accompany steamed lobster. I enjoy using different citrus fruit on fish and shellfish in various guises. Grapefruit and lime are wonderful simply sliced, peeled, and chopped into a salsa or mixed into a seviche marinade. Washing a lime and grating the peel into some walnut or olive oil results in a sauce that can bathe a freshly-cooked trout with an unmatched luminescence and flavour.

Citrus is often combined with other flavours, as in *alla picatta* (lemon caper butter). In *alla picatta*, butter is melted in a pan, some lemon juice is squeezed in, and the two ingredients are whisked together over heat for a minute or two. Then a small amount of capers is thrown in, warmed, and immediately poured over cooked fish. Pan-roasted hake or sole are particularly good partners with this sauce.

Dill

Salmon and dill are natural partners. This stems from the old Scandinavian tradition of *Gravlax*, where a filet of salmon is cured for several days in salt, sugar, dill (or other herbs), and sometimes aquavit or vodka until it becomes "cured" and ready to eat. With the advent of *nouvelle cuisine* in France in the 1970s, the marriage of dill and cream was consummated.

TECHNIQUE TIDBIT
Clarified butter is a butter that has had the milk solids removed so that only the pure butter fat remains. This is very easy to achieve; simply warm butter over medium heat until the fat separates and rises to the top, about 10 minutes. Then carefully pour off the golden elixir, preferably through a fine strainer. Discard the creamy milk solids.

Dill Cream Sauce

Yield ❧ 2 cups (500 ml)

This sauce is a simple yet rich adornment to its classic match, salmon. It would also be great with Arctic char or sea trout.

1 Tbsp (15 ml) butter
1 shallot, minced
1 clove garlic, minced
1 cup (250 ml) Sauvignon Blanc, or
    other white wine
3 cups (750 ml) heavy cream
pinch of salt
Tabasco, to taste
1 Tbsp (15 ml) chopped fresh dill

Melt the butter in a mid-sized saucepan. Add the minced shallot, and sweat over medium heat until translucent.

Add the garlic and cook an additional 2–3 minutes—do not brown.

Add the wine and reduce until only ¼ cup (60 ml) is left, about 10 minutes.

Add the cream and reduce by ⅓, or until there is approximately 2 cups (500 ml) of liquid. Be careful the cream does not boil over; reduce heat if it does so.

Remove from heat and stir in the salt, Tabasco, and dill. Whisk thoroughly and serve immediately, or freeze for future use.

To freeze, pour the cooled sauce into a large zipper storage bag that can hold the sauce easily. To thaw, peel off and discard the bag and reheat the sauce in a double boiler, whisking often.

Extra Virgin Olive Oil

Perhaps my favourite "sauce" for fish, olive oil is making a resurgence worldwide, not just for its flavour, but also for the proven health benefits of monounsaturated fatty acids, high levels of vitamin E, and antioxidants.

As a sauce for fish, olive oil is a popular choice in most Mediterranean countries, where it is occasionally mixed with fresh herbs and drizzled over cooked seafood.

Each of the many varieties of excellent olive oils from all over the world lend a different flavour profile to seafood. A Tuscan light and peppery extra virgin olive oil whisked with grated lemon peel goes well with shrimp. At Tempest, we create a lemon chive vinaigrette that we use as a sauce for our grilled halibut.

There are various degrees of quality when it comes to olive oil. High-quality oils from places like Italy, France, and California are rich in flavour and are best used to dress fish or finish a dish. Lighter oils are better for cooking. Olive oil labelled "pomace" oil is oil made by pressing the olive seeds after the extra virgin oil has been extracted. It is less expensive and a good alternative to vegetable oils for cooking. Generally, the darker green the oil is, the richer and fruitier it will be. Major supermarkets and quality boutique food shops will invariably carry several types of oil in all price ranges.

Saffron, Tomato, and Olive Oil Ragout

Yield ✑ about 2 cups (500 ml)

I recommend using a rich, fruity olive oil from Spain or Greece for the following recipe.

½ tsp (2 ml) saffron threads
4 ripe tomatoes, seeded and quartered
2 roasted red peppers, peeled and seeded
2 marinated artichoke hearts, roughly chopped
1 red onion, sliced
4 green or black olives, pitted and roughly chopped
3 cloves garlic, minced
2 Tbsp (30 ml) lemon juice
½ cup (100 ml) white wine
½ cup (100 ml) extra virgin olive oil
6 fresh basil leaves, thinly sliced
salt and pepper, to taste

Combine all the ingredients in a heavy saucepan on the stove. Bring to a boil, reduce heat to low, then simmer 5 minutes, or until tomatoes and onions are softened. Reserve warm.

Beurre Blanc

The gold standard of French sauces for fish and shellfish is the French beurre blanc. A chef is said to be accomplished in French culinary culture when he or she can consistently make a beurre blanc without it breaking. (Breaking occurs when the fat separates from the other ingredients, resulting in a scrambled egg texture, rather than a velvety smooth sauce.)

A beurre blanc is made by reducing wine (usually white, but red is becoming increasingly popular) and chopped shallots until the liquid has almost completely evaporated, then whisking in butter a little at a time over fairly high heat, thus emulsifying it. Flavouring agents can be added at the end.

Orange Beurre Blanc

Yield ❧ about 1 ½ cups (300 ml)

1 orange
1 cup (250 ml) fruity white wine, like muscat
   or Chardonnay
1 tsp (5 ml) butter + 1 cup (250 ml) unsalted
   butter, cut into ½-inch (1-cm) cubes
1 shallot, minced
1 clove garlic, minced
1 Tbsp (15 ml) heavy cream
pinch of salt
Tabasco, to taste

Zest the orange with a zester or grater and reserve the zest. Juice the orange and strain out any seeds. Add the juice to the white wine and reserve.

In a medium saucepan, sweat the shallot in 1 tsp (5 ml) of butter for 3 minutes. Add the garlic and cook 2 more minutes—do not brown.

Deglaze with the white wine/juice mixture and add the zest. Reduce the liquid until only 2 tablespoons (30 ml) remain.

Whisk in the cream (it acts as a stabilizer for the beurre blanc so that it is less likely to break). Steadily whisk in the butter, one cube at a time, only adding another cube when the first one has just melted. The sauce should stay just below a boil while the butter is added. Do not add the butter too quickly—it should take you about 4–5 minutes. When the butter has been incorporated, remove the sauce from the heat and stir in the salt and Tabasco. Keep the sauce in a warm (not hot) place until ready to serve.

Hollandaise

While most of us know hollandaise as the topping of choice for our Sunday morning eggs Benedict, it is also a traditional fish sauce. Salmon and asparagus with hollandaise has graced many tables over the centuries since its invention. Rich and decadent, hollandaise is a variation on beurre blanc, with the addition of egg yolks. Instead of being cut in cubes and whipped in cold, the butter is clarified (page 11) and whisked in warm, creating a velvety texture in balance with a rich fish. Additional ingredients can be added to a hollandaise in order to create another sauce—adding tomato and tomato paste for example, creates chôron sauce.

Fruit and Seafood

To this day I continue to cook at the Green Turtle Club in Abaco, Bahamas, where I am the consulting executive chef. There is an amazing array of seafood available, completely different than what is available in Atlantic Canada. One of the techniques that I developed there was to combine seafood with fruit, and not just citrus. Most fruit has an inherent sweetness but also a counterbalancing acidity that marries well to fish and shellfish. It lends an exoticism to seafood that we are unused to here in northeastern North America. The marriage of tropical fruit and fish is to be celebrated and explored whenever possible.

Fruits that lend themselves to puréed or cooked sauces include mangos, passion fruits, guavas, cherries, and peaches. Peeled, chopped roughly, and puréed in a blender with a few simple ingredients, these fruits can lift a piece of grilled red snapper or albacore tuna to the realm of the divine.

Warm Mango Coulis

Yield ✎ 2 cups (500 ml)

I used this as our house sauce for grilled fish like wahoo, hog snapper, grouper, and mahi mahi when I was at the Green Turtle Club. Mangos were plentiful and the brightly tropical flavour, along with the hint of heat from the jalapeno, was a great complement to the smoky flavours of the grilled fish. To vary the heat and flavour, try substituting a bird pepper, Thai chile, or hot red chile for the jalapeno.

1 Tbsp (15 ml) extra virgin olive oil
1 medium onion, peeled and chopped
1 clove garlic
1 jalapeno pepper, seeded and diced
salt and pepper, to taste
1 large, very ripe mango, peeled and chopped
1 tsp (5 ml) sugar or honey
⅔ cup (150 ml) white wine
1 cup (200 ml) water, vegetable stock
   or light fish stock
2 Tbsp (30 ml) lemon or lime juice
1 Tbsp (15 ml) butter

Warm the oil in a medium skillet. Add the onion, garlic, and jalapeno. Season with salt and pepper, and cook for 5 minutes. Add the mango and cook an additional 3 minutes, or until the mango begins to soften. Remove from heat and cool briefly.

Add the mango mixture, sugar or honey, wine, water or stock, and citrus juice to a large blender with a tight-fitting lid. With a towel over the top of the blender and your hand bearing down so the lid cannot pop off, pulse the blender for a few very short bursts. (If hot liquids are blended without pulsing to get the liquids moving, the steam created can blow the top off the blender and splatter the sauce all over.)

Increase the length of the bursts until there seems to be an inclination for the top of the blender to pop off. Hit the lowest blend setting on the blender and purée the mix for 2 minutes or until it is completely smooth. The sauce should be easily pourable. If it is too thick, add a little water or stock.

Pour the sauce back into a clean saucepan and slowly bring it to a simmer. Whisk in the butter and taste the sauce for seasoning. Add more salt and Tabasco if necessary. Reserve for use.

Salsas, Condiments, and Chutneys

The salsa we all know best comes from Mexican cuisine and is redolent with tomato, jalapeno, cilantro, and onion. But many variations on salsas and chutneys are excellent with fish and shellfish. Fruits that are adaptable for salsas and chutneys include pears, peaches, starfruits, papayas, kumquats, strawberries, bananas (especially in combination with curry), kiwis, pomegranates, and pineapples. I particularly enjoy making raw fruit salsas that include an element of heat (chile peppers, habaneros, etc.), a member of the allium family (onions, green onions, chives, and/or garlic), some fresh ginger, and tomato or roasted red pepper for colour and texture. Cilantro is often included in a salsa, but can be replaced by basil, mint, Italian parsley, or whatever tickles your fancy.

Avocado Salsa

Yield ⤳ about 2 cups (500 ml)

1 small red onion, minced
2 cloves garlic, minced
1 ripe tomato, peeled, seeded, and diced
4 sprigs cilantro, chopped stems and all
1 Tbsp (15 ml) fresh lime juice
1 jalapeno pepper, seeded and diced
2 Tbsp (30 ml) extra virgin olive oil
2 ripe avocados, peeled, seeded,
   and finely diced
salt and pepper, to taste

Combine all the ingredients except the avocados and salt and pepper in a large bowl, and toss thoroughly. Fold the avocado in gently so the flesh does not break up any further. Add salt and pepper to taste (the avocado benefits from a healthy dose of salt), and if desired add a little more olive oil at the end to moisten the mixture. It should have the texture of tomato salsa. Use within 24 hours. If storing overnight, gently place a piece of cling film directly on the surface of the salsa to help retard browning.

Tropical Fruit Salsa

Yield ✎ about 2 cups (500 ml)

This salsa is particularly well-suited to fish like mahi mahi, halibut, or tuna. Fish grilled over a wood flame, topped with the salsa below and served with steamed basmati rice, is a meal I relish at any time of the year. The pickled ginger, sometimes called sushi ginger, can be picked up in the Asian aisle, or shelf, of most supermarkets, or in specialty Asian food shops.

1 ripe medium papaya, peeled and chopped
    into ¼-inch (½-cm) dice
1 ripe medium mango, peeled and cut into
    ¼-inch (½-cm) dice
1 small red onion, peeled and minced
3 Tbsp (45 ml) cilantro
3 stems green onion, chopped
1 Tbsp (15 ml) lime juice
1 Tbsp (15 ml) sesame oil
1 Tbsp (15 ml) canola oil
1 Tbsp (15 ml) minced ginger
1 Tbsp (15 ml) pickled ginger
1 Tbsp (15 ml) garlic
sugar, to taste
salt and pepper, to taste

Combine all the ingredients in a large bowl. Let the flavours mingle for one hour before serving.

Char

ARCTIC CHAR IS AN INCREASINGLY POPULAR fish that is a perfect substitute for farmed Atlantic salmon. It is rich in antioxidants and essential omega-3 oils. It grills well, both whole or in fillets, and can be cured or smoked with great success.

A number of years ago in Nova Scotia, an enterprising band of Mi'kmaq secured federal funding to farm Arctic char near Truro, creating the company Nova Scotia Arctic Char. Ten years later, they have joined forces with a company from northern Canada, Icy Waters, and are now one of the largest suppliers of Arctic char in North America.

Seared Arctic Char with Sauerkraut and Cider Reduction

Yield ⁀ 6 servings

Char's light texture lends itself well to the flavours of sauerkraut and cider. If char is not available, sea trout or rainbow trout can provide a good substitute.

6 portions Arctic char filet (5.3 oz/150 g each)
2 Tbsp (30 ml) extra virgin olive oil,
   or grapeseed oil
salt and pepper, to taste
4 cups (1 litre) prepared sauerkraut
2 Tbsp (30 ml) + 2 cups (500 ml) apple cider
½ cup (100 ml) water
½ cup (100 ml) apple cider vinegar
½ cup (100 ml) L' Acadie Blanc,
   or other white wine
2 Tbsp (30 ml) butter
Tabasco, to taste
18 small new potatoes

Place the filets on a platter large enough to hold them in a single layer. Drizzle them with half of the oil and season them with salt and pepper on both sides. Marinate the filets for one hour in the fridge.

Boil the potatoes until they are soft, then drain and cool.

Place the sauerkraut in a strainer and rinse it once with fresh cool water. Allow it to drain over the sink for half an hour. Place the sauerkraut in a saucepan with the 2 Tbsp (30 ml) apple cider and water, and bring to a simmer over low heat. Place the potatoes on top of the sauerkraut and sprinkle a little salt over everything. Place a lid over the pot and cook until the liquid has evaporated and the potatoes are hot—about 15 minutes. Check occasionally to ensure that the liquid is not gone and the sauerkraut is not scorching. Separate the sauerkraut and potatoes when they are finished cooking.

While the sauerkraut is heating, prepare the sauce. Combine the 2 cups (500 ml) of cider, cider vinegar, and wine in a saucepan over medium-high heat. Reduce until approximately one cup remains, then whisk in the butter. This should take about 10 minutes. Reserve in a warm place.

In a large nonstick skillet, heat the remaining oil over medium-high heat. Sear the fish on the first side until a slightly crunchy crust starts to form— look for a little browning on the visible edges of the fish. Flip the char over carefully with a fish flipper and cook 2 more minutes on the other side. Remove from heat.

Serve a portion of the sauerkraut into a large-rimmed soup bowl. Top with a piece of fish. Place 3 potatoes around the fish and drizzle the sauce overtop. Serve immediately.

Clams

CLAMS ARE OMNIPRESENT ALONG THE
Northeastern seaboard. Soft shells, like the famous
"steamers" at Woodman's Restaurant in Essex,
Massachusetts; giant quahogs, with meat that is sweet
but chewy; and littlenecks, which are often steamed in
wine and tossed with fresh pasta are all readily available
here. Most Maritimers have either gone clam digging
and enjoyed their gritty yet delicious spoils steamed right
there on the beach, enjoyed a cup of fresh clam chowder,
or tasted fried clam strips.

Linguini with Littlenecks and Garlic (Linguini alla Vongole)

Yield ☙ 6 servings

I particularly love small hardshell clam varieties like littleneck and mahogany. Though they are delicious raw with just a little lemon juice and Tabasco, I prefer this method of light steaming and tossing them in fresh pasta. Though freshly made pasta is preferable, a good-quality dry linguini, fettuccine, spaghetti, or tagliatelle can be substituted. If you can find or make squid ink linguini, even better! Don't be frightened by the amount of garlic here—the flavour is huge and the vampires will stay away.

SERVE WITH
a good Italian Pinot Grigio or Soave

16 oz (500 g) fresh linguini, or other long pasta
1 tsp (5 ml) + 1 tsp (5 ml) + 2 tsp (10 ml)
  extra virgin olive oil
8 cloves garlic, minced
1 tsp (5 ml) chile flakes
2 ¼ lbs (1 kg) fresh littleneck or mahogany
  clams (or other small hardshell clams),
  washed thoroughly
1 cup (200 ml) white wine
1 Tbsp (15 ml) lemon juice
1 large fresh ripe tomato, peeled,
  seeded, and diced
3 Tbsp (45 ml) chopped Italian parsley

Fill a large pot with salted water and 1 tsp (5 ml) of olive oil. Add the linguini and boil until cooked. Al dente (firm but not hard) consistency is desired as you will cook the pasta some more with the clams.

When the pasta is cooked, drain it, but reserve 2 cups of the cooking water. Toss the noodles with 1 more tsp (5 ml) of olive oil to keep them from sticking and reserve them nearby in a large metal bowl.

In a large skillet able to hold the pasta, warm the remaining 2 tsp (10 ml) of the olive oil and add the garlic, chile flakes, and clams, and cook over medium heat, stirring regularly for 3–4 minutes, or until the clams just start to open.

Add the wine and lemon juice and cover the skillet with a lid or some foil. Steam the clams for 1–2 minutes, or until they are open, whichever comes first. You want to be careful not to overcook them.

Remove the lid, add the cooked pasta, tomato, and parsley and enough of the reserved pasta water to make a loose broth. Stir in the remaining olive oil, add salt and pepper as desired, and divide immediately among 6 plates or bowls.

Pour any of the broth remaining in the skillet over the pasta. Italians do not typically add parmigiano or Parmesan cheese to seafood dishes, but should you desire, please do so.

Crispy Fried Clams and Apple Tartar Sauce

Yield ❧ 6 servings

Years ago, when my wife's sister Sara and her new husband visited Nova Scotia for the first time, we rode the ferry from Chester out to Big Tancook Island and spent a cloudless July day exploring the island. Just before returning to Chester, we stopped at a little canteen and ordered clam strips and fries. Those hot, crispy, salty clams, cooked and consumed seconds later, remain one of my favourite food memories. I have added some crispy apple to a traditional tartar sauce recipe for a little extra crunch. This sauce is excellent with any kind of fried fish or shellfish. For speedy cooking, pre-purchased, frozen clam strips can be substituted for the steamer clams. Just make sure that they are not pre-breaded.

Apple Tartar Sauce
1 cup (250 ml) mayonnaise
2 tsp (10 ml) lemon juice
1 tsp (5 ml) garlic
2 Tbsp (30 ml) capers
1 large kosher dill pickle, finely diced
1 tsp (5 ml) Dijon mustard
1 Tbsp (30 ml) sour cream
1 tsp (5 ml) sugar
salt and white pepper, to taste
1 small Jonagold apple, peeled, cored, and
    finely diced

Crispy Fried Clams
5 lbs (2.3 kg) steamer clams
4 eggs
Tabasco, to taste
2 cups (500 ml) flour
1 tsp (5 ml) seasoning salt or sea salt

countertop fryer or large pot of oil heated to
    360°F (180°C)

To make the sauce, combine all ingredients and chill for 1–2 hours to allow flavours to meld.

To make the clams, preheat a countertop fryer (or very large pot) to 360°F (180°C) and fill with just over 3 inches (8 cm) of canola oil.

Steam the clams in salted water or seawater. Strain and place in an ice bath until the clams are cooled. Remove from the water and drain. Shuck the clams and remove all the guts except the bellies and strips, though the bellies can also be removed if you are not fond of them.

Beat the eggs and the Tabasco in a large bowl. In a separate large bowl, mix the flour and the seasoning salt.

Place the clams in the egg mixture and then with a slotted spoon or stir fry basket (often called a spider) drain off the egg and place the clams in the flour. Shake them around thoroughly to coat. Clean the spoon and dry it, then use it to lift the clams out of the flour. Shake off any excess flour and place the clams in the fryer to cook for about 4 minutes maximum, until golden brown. Make sure the frying clams don't stick to one another. Drain the clams on a paper towel, sprinkle them with some sea salt, and serve immediately with lemon and the Apple Tartar Sauce.

Razor Clams and Celeriac Napoleon

Yield ☙ 4 servings

This was a signature dish at The Everest Room in Chicago. Razor Clams from Maine would show up three or four times a year and Chef Joho always had me prepare this dish. The dish requires some degree of fussing, but it uses very simple ingredients. "Napoleon" in the title simply refers to a layered stack of food, which in this case is the celeriac and clams. Note that you can also substitute regular clam strips for the razor clams.

36 razor clams

2 cups (500 ml) fish stock, vegetable stock, or
 salted water

a squeeze of lemon juice

½ tsp (2 ml) salt

1 head celeriac, peeled, sliced very thin, and
 cut into 2-inch × 2-inch (5-cm × 5-cm)
 squares (about 16 pieces)

2 cups (500 ml) Vin Blanc Sauce (see
 note below)

6 chives, finely chopped

Vin Blanc Sauce

This is exactly the same recipe as the Dill Cream Sauce (page 12) but the dill is kept out of the recipe and an additional 2 Tbsp (30 ml) of butter is whisked in at the end of cooking.

With a sharp knife, open the clams. The desirable edible portion of the clam is the opaque white part about 1–2 inches long—similar to a clam strip in a regular clam. Remove the strips and guts from the clams and discard the guts. Rinse the razor clam strips thoroughly and reserve.

Combine the stock or salted water, lemon juice, and salt in a large pot and bring to a boil over high heat. Add the squares of celeriac. Reduce the heat to low and poach the celeriac for about 5 minutes, or until it is tender, but not falling apart. Drain, and reserve warm.

Place the Vin Blanc Sauce in a pot and warm over medium heat. Add the clam strips and poach the clams in the sauce until they are just cooked through, about 3 minutes. Stir in the chives.

On a serving plate, place a warm square of celeriac. Top with 3 clam strips and some sauce. Repeat twice more, then top with a final sheet of celeriac. Repeat with the remaining servings. Finish by drizzling some sauce over the top. Serve immediately.

Crab

CRAB IS NOT AS COMMONLY EATEN IN CANADA as it is in the United States. Crab cakes from Maryland, crab gumbo from Louisiana, and steamed crab claws from Florida are all indigenous foods that appeal to tourists and locals alike. But crab is readily available in Atlantic Canada. I would suggest buying shelled crab meat. If you are keen you can steam and clean you own crabs, but this is a very laborious process. Nonetheless, always check cleaned crab meat for bits of shell or cartilage before eating or cooking.

Spicy Caribbean Crab Cakes

Yields ⌒ 6 servings (about 12 large crab cakes)

These are always a hit at the restaurant, and when made into small bite-size mini-cakes they are excellent canapés for a dinner party. Panko is a Japanese bread crumb that can be found at Asian markets.

SERVE WITH

Warm Mango Coulis (page 16) and some sprigs of cilantro for garnish

2 Tbsp (30 ml) olive or vegetable oil

1 shallot, peeled and chopped

1 medium red pepper, finely diced

1 medium yellow pepper, finely diced

1 large jalapeno pepper or red finger pepper, chopped and seeds removed (or left in depending on heat preference)

1 small red onion, peeled and finely diced

¾ inch (2 cm) ginger, peeled and finely chopped

4 cloves garlic, chopped

1 lb (500 g) cooked lump rock crab or snow crab meat

4 Tbsp (60 ml) chopped cilantro

1 cup (250 ml) mayonnaise

2 eggs, lightly beaten

1 Tbsp (15 ml) Dijon mustard

1 cup (200 ml) finely diced ripe mango

liberal dashes of Caribbean hot sauce, or Tabasco

salt and pepper, to taste

2 cups (500 ml) + ½ cup (100 ml) panko bread crumbs, or regular bread crumbs

Warm the oil in a large skillet over medium heat. Add the shallot, peppers, hot pepper, red onion, and ginger. Sweat for 5 minutes. Add the garlic and cook for 2 more minutes. Remove to a large bowl and allow to cool for 10 minutes.

Add the remaining ingredients to the bowl, reserving the ½ cup (100 ml) of bread crumbs. Fold the crab cake mixture gently, trying not to break up the lumps of crab meat too much. After the mixture is thoroughly combined, refrigerate for one hour.

Remove the crab cake mixture from the fridge. Spread the remaining 100 ml of bread crumbs on a cookie sheet. Form the crab mixture into balls slightly larger than golf balls, then flatten them out so that each cake resembles a small hockey puck. Dredge all sides in the bread crumbs. (You can reserve the crab cakes for cooking later, as they can be refrigerated for up to 24 hours.)

There are 2 options for cooking the cakes. You can bake them in a 425°F (220°C) oven for 12–15 minutes, flipping them after 8 minutes, or you can pan-fry or deep-fry the cakes in some 360°F (180°C) oil until golden brown and crunchy, about 3 minutes.

Crab Soufflé

Yield ☙ 6 appetizer soufflés

I invented this dish while in the Bahamas. Stone crabs regenerate their claws so the accepted method of harvesting them is to remove one claw and put the crab back in the sea, leaving it with one claw to defend itself while the other one grows back. This is a good example of sustainable harvesting happening at a grassroots level. My friend Dale Roberts has been a successful stone crab fisherman in the Abacos for years. Every two weeks Dale would bring us 100 pounds of the freshest claws you could imagine, some of them weighing over a pound each. They were delicious simply steamed and served with lemon butter, but we needed a way to make them more refined to suit the elegance of the Green Turtle Club's dining room, touted as the best in the Bahamas for many years. Once I perfected this recipe they were immensely popular, and I have been making this soufflé ever since. Gruyère is really the only cheese that has the right flavour profile for this dish but a Gouda or Swiss cheese will do in a pinch.

1 Tbsp (15 ml) + ¼ cup (50 g) butter

2 Tbsp (30 ml) + ½ cup (100 ml) flour

2 shallots, minced

2 cloves garlic, minced

2 cups (500 ml) whole milk, room temperature or warmer

½ cup (100 ml) white wine

½ lb (200 g) Comté Gruyère cheese, grated

½ tsp (2 ml) nutmeg

½ tsp (2 ml) paprika

salt and Tabasco, to taste

¼ cup (50 ml) Dijon mustard

4 eggs separated, yolks beaten with a whisk until pale yellow

1 lb (500 g) picked-over crab meat

6 (8 oz/225 g) straight-sided soufflé dishes

Rub the 1 Tbsp (15 ml) of butter over the inside of the soufflé dishes, then dredge them with the 2 Tbsp (30 ml) flour, making sure all sides of the dishes are covered. Shake out any excess flour and set aside.

In a large pot, melt the ¼ cup (50 g) butter over medium heat and add the shallots. Cook for 5 minutes, stirring often. Add the garlic and cook an additional 3 minutes, continuing to stir often. Add the ½ cup (100 ml) flour and stir to combine. You are making a roux. Cook for 3–4 minutes, stirring constantly to avoid sticking. Add the warm milk and wine and cook until the mixture starts to thicken. Add the cheese, nutmeg, paprika, salt, Tabasco, and mustard. Remove from the heat and stir until the cheese has melted, about 4 minutes. The mixture should have the consistency of soft pizza dough. Let cool briefly then add the egg yolks, stirring in thoroughly. Continue to let cool to room temperature, about 15 minutes.

When the soufflé base is cool, whip the egg whites in a mixer until they form soft peaks. Fold half of the whites into the soufflé base. Fold in the crab meat and disperse throughout the base evenly. Finally, gently fold in the remaining egg whites. Carefully divide the mixture among the 6 soufflé dishes and fill to just below the rim of the dish, making sure the tops are smooth. Run the tip of your thumb just around the top of the inside edge of the dish to create a tiny groove between the soufflé and the side of the dish.

Place the soufflé dishes on a level sheet tray and place in a 375°F (190°C) oven for 20 minutes, or until they have risen less than ½ inch (about 1 cm) above the edge of the dish. The soufflé should be golden brown on top and firm in the middle. Serve immediately.

Crab and Heart of Palm Salad

Yield ☙ 6 servings

This is a great salad for a summer dinner party on the deck. It can be made ahead and kept in the fridge until serving time. Canned heart of palm is available in virtually all grocery stores. It has a refreshing flavour and great texture. A quick garnish with some sprigs of arugula or parsley, a drizzle of good olive oil, and off you go.

SERVE WITH
a refreshing Sancerre or Chenin Blanc

1 cup (200 ml) mayonnaise

2 Tbsp (30 ml) lemon juice

1 shallot, finely chopped

1 clove garlic, minced

2 stalks green onion, chopped

1 roasted red pepper, peeled, seeded, and diced

salt and pepper, to taste

paprika, to taste

1.10 lb (500 g) cleaned crab meat

2 cans heart of palm, drained and dried, cut into sticks the size of french fries

1–2 Tbsp (15–30 ml) extra virgin olive oil, for drizzling

fresh greens (e.g. arugula), for garnish

Mix the mayonnaise, lemon juice, shallot, garlic, green onion, red pepper, salt and pepper, and paprika together in a large bowl. Gently fold in the crab meat. Allow the flavours to meld for 1–2 hours.

Dress the hearts of palm with the olive oil and arrange them decoratively on a plate, laying 3 pieces down side by side on each plate. Divide the crab salad into 6 equal portions. Place half of one portion on top of the heart of palm pieces. Place 3 more pieces of heart of palm on top of the crab and then the remaining portion of crab on top. Repeat on the 5 remaining plates.

At serving time, drizzle some olive oil over the top, and garnish the plates with fresh green leaves—arugula, parsley, or chervil.

Haddock

THE MOIST, DELICATE TEXTURE OF HADDOCK and its delicate flavour make it a perennial favourite in the Maritimes and New England.

ETHICAL EATING NOTE
Haddock is still relatively plentiful in our oceans. Whenever possible, ask for line-caught or day-boat haddock that has been fished sustainably. This will help to create an environment that will preserve global fish stocks for years to come.

The Best Fish and Chips

Yield ∾ 6 servings

Tempura batter is the secret to a light, crispy crust that keeps the fish moist inside after frying. I recommend investing in a countertop fryer, readily available at most department stores. Make sure the fish is very dry before dipping it in a tempura batter. To make this really easy, you can use store-bought tempura batter, but instead of adding water, use sparkling water or club soda. As for the fries, have you ever wondered how fast food joints and some restaurants have such crispy fries? It's because they cook them in a two-part process: a low-temperature blanch and the final high-temperature fry.

SERVE WITH
Apple Tartar Sauce (page 25)

Chips
3 large baking potatoes, washed thoroughly and dried

countertop fryer or large pot of oil heated to 300°F (150°C)

Tempura-Battered Fish
1 medium egg
1 cup (200 ml) cold sparkling water, club soda, or tap water
½ cup (100 g) plain flour
12 portions haddock filet (5 oz/100 g each), patted dry
sea salt, to taste
1 lemon, sliced (optional)

TECHNIQUE TIDBIT
Instead of regular club soda, try a sparkling water flavoured with lemon or lime. This will imbue the batter with a delicious hit of taste.

Heat the oil to 300°F (150°C) in a fryer or pot. Cut the potatoes lengthwise into shoestring-size pieces. Prepare a large sheet tray covered in paper towel and place it near the fryer. In batches that do not overcrowd the fryer, cook the shoestring potato fries for 4–5 minutes, until they just begin to colour. Remove the potatoes from the oil and place them on the paper towel. (This process is called blanching and results in the crispiest fries.) Repeat with the remaining potatoes and let the fries cool. After the potatoes are cool, discard the paper towel. Reserve the fries until you are ready for the high-temperature fry.

Prepare the batter immediately before use. Reheat oil to 350°F (180°C). Beat the egg in a bowl and add the cold water. (The water must be as cold as possible, as this prevents the batter from absorbing too much oil, keeping it light and crispy.)

Lightly mix in the flour with a fork and beat gently. Don't worry too much about lumps. Dip the fish pieces into the batter and allow most of it to come off. Only a very thin layer of batter should remain on the fish. Place 1–2 pieces of fish in the fryer carefully and cook 5 minutes, or until golden brown and

crispy. Make sure that you do not crowd the fish in the fryer. Remove the fried fish to a tray covered with paper towel and sprinkle with some sea salt. Repeat with remaining fish. Place in a hot oven for a couple of minutes while you finish the fries.

In small batches, drop the potatoes into the now hot oil and cook until crispy, 1–2 minutes. Remove the fries from oil to a paper towel-covered tray and season with sea salt.

Serve the fish on top of the chips with a slice of lemon, some Apple Tartar Sauce, and maybe some malt vinegar in traditional English style.

Halibut

HALIBUT IS PERHAPS MY FAVOURITE FISH. It holds up well to most cooking methods, has a great firm texture, and flakes perfectly when cooked properly. Its flavour is rich yet somehow subtle, and both assertive flavours (like miso or soy) and delicate ones (like rosewater or shrimp broth) can be used to scent this wonder of the sea.

Provençale Seafood Stew with Halibut, Shrimp, and Mussels

Yield ☙ 4–6 servings

This rich soup/stew is my interpretation of the famous bouillabaisse from the south of France. In this recipe I punch up the anise flavour with the addition of both fennel and Pernod. These licorice notes marry very well with the saffron and orange flavours redolent throughout. Served with a crusty loaf and a crisp glass of white or rosé wine, this is hearty enough for a winter warmer but is equally at home if dining alfresco in the late summer.

SERVE WITH
croutes (baguette sliced, brushed with olive oil, and toasted)

16 large shrimp, peeled and deveined, shells reserved

4 cups (1 litre) water or fish stock

1 tsp (5 ml) saffron

2 Tbsp (30 ml) + 1–2 Tbsp (15–30 ml) extra virgin olive oil

1 bulb fennel, chopped, fronds reserved for garnish

1 large onion, chopped

1 large carrot, peeled and chopped + 1 large carrot, peeled and cubed

2 stalks celery, chopped

½ cup (100 ml) tomato paste

5 cloves garlic, minced

red chile flakes, pinch

½ cup (100 ml) Pernod, sambuca, or ouzo

1 cup (250 ml) white wine

4 cups (1 litre) fish stock

2 oranges, zested and juiced

4 bay leaves

6 sprigs fresh thyme

1 (19 oz/500 ml) can of plum tomatoes, chopped

1 large baking potato, peeled and cubed (or 12 new potatoes, halved)

1.10 lbs (500 g) halibut, or other white fish, chopped

12 medium scallops

16 mussels

salt and pepper, to taste

Tabasco, to taste

butter, to taste

fennel fronds, for garnish

chives, for garnish

Roasted Red Pepper Aioli (Rouille)

1 roasted red pepper, seeded and peeled

1 egg

1 tsp (5 ml) minced garlic

1 tsp (5 ml) lemon juice

salt and pepper, to taste

sugar, to taste

Tabasco, to taste

1 cup (250 ml) olive oil

Bring the shrimp shells and water to a boil. Reduce the heat and simmer for half an hour. Strain and discard the shells. Add the saffron to the liquid. Reserve this shrimp stock.

Warm the 2 Tbsp (30 ml) of olive oil in a large pot over medium heat. Add the fennel and mirepoix (onion, chopped carrot, and celery) and sweat for 10–15 minutes. Add the tomato paste and cook 5 minutes, stirring regularly. Add the garlic and chile flakes and cook for another 5 minutes. Add the Pernod, sambuca, or ouzo (it may flame) and cook for 2 minutes. Add the wine and stir. Add the fish stock, shrimp/saffron stock, orange juice and zest, bay leaves, thyme, and canned tomatoes. Simmer for half an hour. Cool briefly.

Carefully purée the mixture in a blender with a towel over the top. Strain and return to the stove. Add the cubed carrot and potato and simmer 15 minutes. Add the fish and simmer 5 minutes. Add the scallops and simmer 4 minutes. Add the shrimp and mussels and simmer 3 minutes. Season with salt, pepper, and Tabasco. Stir in the butter.

To prepare the rouille, place all the ingredients except the oil in a blender, and purée. Add a little water if the mixture is too thick. With the blender running, carefully add the oil in a thin stream until it is incorporated and the mixture is thick. Season the rouille with more salt and pepper, and add as much Tabasco as you desire—it should have a bit of zip!

Serve the stew in large bowls with croutes, rouille, and fennel fronds, and drizzle with the remaining oil and chopped chives.

TECHNIQUE TIDBIT

To roast red peppers:

Brush the red peppers with some olive oil and place them on a barbecue, or in a 400°F (200°C) oven. Roast them for 10 minutes, or until the skin is puffed and charred. Remove the peppers with tongs, place them in a container with a lid, seal, and let them steam for 10 minutes. Then carefully peel and seed the peppers.

Grilled Halibut with Fingerling Potatoes, Baby Spinach, and Roasted Red Peppers

Yield ☙ 6 servings

A most elegant dish, this is easy to prepare yet the results are sure to impress even the most discerning diner. Marinate the fish in some olive oil and salt and pepper for an hour in the fridge before cooking. Some time spent chopping the veggies and tomatoes into nice even cubes is what can make this dish restaurant quality. Visit a kitchen supply store to find 3-inch ring moulds, or make your own by cutting the top and bottom off an empty tuna can.

Marinade
2 Tbsp (30 ml) olive oil
½ tsp (2 ml) each salt and pepper

Herb Vinaigrette
1 tsp (5 ml) chopped fresh chives
1 tsp (5 ml) chopped fresh thyme,
    stems removed
1 Tbsp (15 ml) chopped fresh Italian Parsley
2 cloves garlic, minced
1 tsp (5 ml) Dijon mustard
3 Tbsp (50 ml) white wine vinegar
1 tsp (5 ml) sugar or honey
salt and pepper, to taste
1 ½ cup (300 ml) extra virgin olive oil

The Essentials
6 pieces of Halibut filet, (5 oz/150 g each)
    or 1 or 2 halibut steaks
12 fingerling or (¾ lb/300 g) new potatoes
2 cloves garlic, minced
2 roasted red peppers, peeled, seeded and cut
    into ½-inch (1-cm) squares

Salad
7 oz (200 g) fresh baby spinach
1 tomato, peeled, seeded and diced into ¼-inch
    (½-cm) cubes
fresh baby greens, mesclun salad, or pea and
    onion shoots, for garnish

Combine the olive oil, salt, and pepper, and marinate the fish in the mixture for 1 hour.

To prepare the vinaigrette, add all the ingredients except the oil to a blender. Purée until relatively smooth, about 1 minute. Slowly add the oil to the running blender in a stream, until it is all incorporated. Remove the vinaigrette to a container or squirt bottle and reserve.

Set the grill to medium and preheat for 5 minutes. In a large skillet on the stove, or on top of the grill, warm some olive oil and sauté the potatoes until they just start to get brown and crispy. Add the garlic and roasted red peppers and sauté another 2–3 minutes, or until the garlic starts to brown. Remove the skillet from heat and reserve.

Spray the grill with non-stick spray or wipe with some oil applied to a towel or brush. Place the fish on the grill and cook for 5 minutes, or until grill marks form and fish will lift easily (do not try to turn too soon or the fish may stick). Turn the fish and cook another 3–5 minutes, or until cooked through. Remove the fish to a plate and keep warm.

Return the skillet to the grill or stove and reheat the potatoes. Add the spinach, a dash of salt and pepper, and a dash of olive oil and toss the vegetables. Gently wilt the spinach, about 1 minute, being careful not to overcook.

Divide the vegetable mixture among 6 serving plates and top each with a piece of fish. Use a ring mould for a clean presentation. Drizzle and surround the fish with the vinaigrette. Carefully place the tomato pieces around the fish and serve. If desired, you can top the fish with fresh baby greens, mesclun salad, or pea or onion shoots for added elegance.

Lobster

AH, THE PROVERBIAL KING OF THE SEAFOOD table. Once considered plebeian and eaten only by the poor, lobster did not have a place at the gourmet's table. Indeed, native North Americans would fertilize their fields with lobsters! These days, lobster is exalted in the kitchens of the world as a gourmet delicacy. Chefs are constantly looking for new and creative ways to prepare lobster. Its rich and succulent flesh is perfectly balanced with lemon butter or a creamy stock-based sauce from the French culinary tradition, or with a fiery chile sauce prevalent in Chinese cuisines.

Grilled Lobster with Shrimp Americaine Sauce

Yield ⌒ 4 servings

Every summer we serve this dish at Tempest when lobsters are plentiful and tourists are looking for a dish a little different than the usual steamed variety found at local lobster suppers. This recipe is surprisingly easy and yet refined enough for a fancy restaurant. A little work is necessary beforehand, but at serving time most of the work is already done.

SERVE WITH
a dry, unoaked Chardonnay

4 lobsters (1.3 lb/600 g each)
2 Tbsp (30 ml) olive oil, for brushing
salt and pepper, to taste

Shrimp Americain Sauce
2 cups (250 ml) lobster stock (page 10)
⅔ cup (150 ml) sherry
½ cup (100 ml) tomato paste
1 sprig fresh thyme
1 cup (200 ml) heavy cream
½ lb (200 ml) small shrimp, cooked, peeled, deveined, and chopped
salt and Tabasco, to taste
1 Tbsp (15 ml) butter

In a steamer or large pot, cook the lobsters for 10 minutes in boiling water, or until cooked but not overdone. Immediately immerse the lobsters in a large pot of ice water to stop them from cooking further. Take them out and dry them.

With a large heavy knife, split the lobsters in half lengthwise and clean out the tomalley (green paste) and any innards that you do not want to eat. Brush the lobsters with oil, salt, and pepper and set them aside while you prepare the sauce.

To prepare the sauce, heat the lobster stock in a 2-quart saucepan over medium high heat and add the sherry, tomato paste, and sprig of thyme. Reduce the liquid by half. Add the cream and again reduce the liquid by half. Reduce the heat to medium and add the shrimp. Season the sauce with salt and Tabasco, and whisk in the butter. Remove the thyme sprig. Reserve in a warm place.

Preheat your grill for 5–10 minutes. Oil the hot grill and grill the lobsters, flesh-side down, for 5 minutes. Flip them over and cook another 3–4 minutes. Remove the lobsters to a plate and top with sauce. Crack the claws and knuckles with a heavy knife or lobster crackers to allow access to the tasty meat.

Lazyman's Lobster with Ginger Beurre Blanc

Yield ✑ 4 servings

This is my ultimate lobster dish. It takes work but for an intimate dinner meant to impress, spend the time to do it right. Imagine a lobster with no mess, no fuss, no bibs! Easily eaten with a fork and knife.

SERVE WITH
a dry Riesling or Gewürztraminer

4 live lobsters (1.3 lb/600 g each)
2 Tbsp (30 ml) olive oil, for drizzling
1 ½ cups (375 ml) Nova Scotia or New
    York Muscat wine, or Alsatian Riesling
    (approximately a half bottle)
3 Tbsp (45 ml) sushi ginger soaking liquid
    (add rice wine vinegar to make up difference
    if necessary)
1 Tbsp (15 ml) heavy cream
½ cup (115 g) cold unsalted butter, cut into
    small cubes
2 Tbsp (30 ml) sushi ginger, julienned
salt and white pepper, to taste
Tabasco, to taste
1 lb (450 g) organic spinach or arugula, stems
    removed
1 Tbsp (15 ml) olive oil

In a large pot of boiling water or steamer, boil or steam the lobsters for 10 minutes. Remove the lobsters from the pot or steamer and shock in ice water until cold.

Carefully de-shell the lobsters, being extra careful to keep the claws whole. Use a towel or rubber gloves to protect your hands while removing the shell bits.

Reserve the tails with the end of the tail shells on. De-shell the knuckles, reserve the antennae, and save the bodies and the remaining shells for lobster stock.

Fan the tails by cutting on the bias (at 45° angles) into 5 or 6 pieces each. Lay out the fanned tails, claws, and knuckles on a sheet tray, drizzle with some olive oil, and reserve.

In a small, heavy saucepan, reduce the wine and ginger juice until approximately 2 Tbsp (30 ml) remain. Add the cream and reduce again until 2 Tbsp (30 ml) remain.

Reduce the heat to medium-high and carefully whisk in the cubed butter one piece at a time, adding another piece only when the last one is fully melted and just starting to bubble. Whisk constantly.

When the butter is incorporated, remove the saucepan from the heat, stir in the julienned ginger, salt, white pepper, and Tabasco, and reserve in a warm place.

Season the lobster with salt and white pepper, and place the tray of lobster in a 450°F (225°C) for 2–3 minutes.

While the lobster is heating, wilt the spinach in a hot pan with olive oil and season with salt and pepper.

Arrange the spinach on a plate, cover it with the fanned tail, and place the remaining lobster pieces on the plate, recreating the shape of the lobster. Drizzle the sauce over the lobster, garnish with seasonal vegetables and serve.

Lobster Corn Chowder

Yield ∾ 10 servings

This is a signature dish at our restaurant and has been on the menu since we opened six years ago. Try to find some yellow corn if possible, instead of the more common (but to my mind a bit too sweet) peaches and cream corn. If you don't have freshly cooked lobster, you can substitute good quality frozen or canned lobster meat. Water can be substituted for the lobster stock but the flavour will not be as intense. Finally, lobster base is concentrated lobster essence and is sometimes available in finer gourmet shops—substitute crab paste or shrimp paste (more readily available in Asian markets).

2 Tbsp (30 ml) + 3 Tbsp (45 ml) butter

2 slices bacon

1 large onion, diced

2 carrots, diced

2 stalks celery, diced

6 ears fresh corn, kernels sliced off and reserved, and 4 ears reserved

2–3 cloves garlic, minced

1 tsp (5 ml) ground thyme

8 cups (2 litres) lobster stock + 4 cups (1 litre) lobster stock, or water (page 10)

3 cans evaporated milk

4 cups (1 litre) 18% cream

2 large potatoes, peeled and diced

4 bay leaves

2 Tbsp (30 ml) + 1 cup (200 ml) sherry

1 red pepper, chopped

salt, pepper and Tabasco, to taste

1 Tbsp (15 ml) finely chopped shallots

1 tsp (5 ml) garlic, chopped

¼ cup (60 ml) wine

1–2 Tbsp (30 ml) lobster base, or shrimp or crab paste

10 oz (about 300 g), lobster meat, chopped and cooked

China cap

In a soup pot, melt 2 Tbsp (30 ml) of butter over medium heat and add the bacon. Cook for 5 minutes or until the bacon is cooked three-quarters of the way through. Do not burn.

Add the onion, carrots, and celery to the bacon and sauté for 5 minutes. Add the corn kernels and sauté for another 5 minutes. Add the garlic and thyme and cook 5 minutes more. At this point the corn should be aromatic and the vegetables translucent.

Add the 8 cups (2 litres) of lobster stock, evaporated milk, cream, potatoes, and bay leaves, and bring the temperature up to a very gentle simmer. Add the reserved ears of corn and the 2 Tbsp (30 ml) of sherry. Cook for 15 minutes, or until the potatoes are soft, and remove the ears. Do not boil.

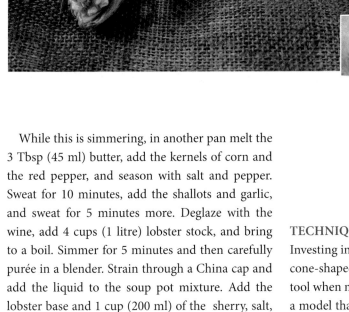

While this is simmering, in another pan melt the 3 Tbsp (45 ml) butter, add the kernels of corn and the red pepper, and season with salt and pepper. Sweat for 10 minutes, add the shallots and garlic, and sweat for 5 minutes more. Deglaze with the wine, add 4 cups (1 litre) lobster stock, and bring to a boil. Simmer for 5 minutes and then carefully purée in a blender. Strain through a China cap and add the liquid to the soup pot mixture. Add the lobster base and 1 cup (200 ml) of the sherry, salt, and Tabasco to taste. When ready to serve, add the chopped lobster meat and heat through.

TECHNIQUE TIDBIT

Investing in a China cap is not inexpensive, but this cone-shaped, fine-mesh strainer is an invaluable tool when making sauces or puréed soups. Look for a model that is made from finely woven mesh steel and has a sturdy handle. In lieu of a China cap, a sieve or strainer will do.

Lobster Fritatta

Yield ❧ 8 servings

This one-pan wonder is great at a brunch, luncheon party or part of a buffet. Equally delicious hot or at room temperature.

SERVE WITH
a light green salad

12 extra large eggs, beaten
1 cup (200 g) Asiago cheese, grated
1 shallot, chopped
2 Tbsp (30 ml) butter
1 cup (200 ml) heavy cream
1 roasted red pepper, peeled, seeded, and
   chopped

6 green onions, chopped
1 lb (500 g) cooked lobster meat, chopped
salt and pepper, to taste
Tabasco, to taste
paprika, to taste

Preheat oven to 200°C (400°F). In a large bowl, whisk eggs and then stir in cheese. Reserve.

In a large (12-inch) non-stick pan, sweat the chopped shallot for 3–4 minutes in the butter. Add the cream and reduce for one minute. Add the red pepper, green onions, lobster, and seasonings. Stir to heat the lobster through. Cool briefly, then stir into the egg mixture. Clean the non-stick pan, then heat over medium heat. Add the egg mixture and cook for 5 minutes. Do not stir! Transfer the pan to the oven and cook until set. (Make sure the handle is oven proof, or wrapped in foil.) Let cool 5 minutes before portioning.

ETHICAL EATING : Free-range organic eggs
Eggs from chickens that have been allowed to pasture and eat natural food are inherently more healthy and nutritious. They have larger, darker yolks and better flavour. Whenever possible, try to visit a farmers' market for your free-range organic eggs or find a farmer that can supply them to you. If free-range eggs are not available, opt for organic eggs, which at least have not had supplements added to their feed.

Mackerel

OUR EAST COAST CULTURE WOULD NOT BE THE same without mackerel. Tinkers, as I was told to call them when we fished the waters off Gooseberry Island in our red dory, were sweet and succulent.

Well, mackerel is not exactly sole—its darker color and assertive oily flavour is, to my mind, an acquired taste that many love and many hate. But it is a most healthy fish to eat, very plentiful in North Atlantic waters, and generally found inshore. Smoking is a very common way to prepare mackerel, but I offer a marinated fish recipe reminiscent of the Mediterranean cultures that marinate anchovies and sardines.

Marinated Mackerel

Yield ☙ 6 servings

This is similar to Solomon Gundy (East Coast-style pickled herring) but a little more refined. Large sardines, rainbow trout, or small red snapper filets could be substituted. Indeed you could treat almost any fish with this marinade—it is a variation of the Escabeche seafood recipes of South and Central America that use any local fish on hand.

4 small mackerel filets (1.3 lbs/600 g total), trimmed of any bones or fins, skin on
salt and white pepper, to taste
2 cups (500 ml) white wine (like Seyval Blanc or Sancerre)
½ cup (100 ml) white wine vinegar
2 shallots, thinly sliced
1 tsp (5 ml) pickled sushi ginger, cut in thin strips
2 carrots, peeled, sliced, and cut into matchsticks
2 lemons, sliced
1 small fresh fennel bulb, top removed, outer layer removed and shaved thinly
1 bay leaf
4 sprigs fresh thyme
12 peppercorns

Make sure that the mackerel filets are well trimmed and there are no bones or fins remaining. Check for pin bones and remove them carefully with a knife, clean needle nose pliers, or tweezers. Cut the filets into 12 equal-size portions and season with salt and white pepper. Place in a glass dish one layer deep, skin-side down.

Combine the other ingredients in a non–reactive saucepan and bring to a boil. Simmer 5 minutes, then immediately pour over the fish and let cool to room temperature.

Cover the glass dish with plastic wrap when cool and place it in the fridge for 12 hours or overnight.

To serve, place the filets on some greens and drizzle some marinade on top.

Monkfish

MONKFISH IS A DELICIOUS FISH, ALTHOUGH one of the ugliest in the sea. Its gigantic head is as wide as the body of the fish is long (think of the anglerfish in *Finding Nemo*) and is almost always disposed of before returning to port.

Monkfish is often referred to as poor man's lobster, as its cooked texture and flavour is similar. Firm-fleshed, it holds up well to grilling and strong marinades. The two recipes here are my favourite ways of preparing it. Be sure to remove as much of the gelatinous outer layer as possible by trimming away any greyish colour with a very sharp knife.

Prosciutto-Wrapped Monkfish with Smoked Tomato Sauce

Yield ⌒ 6 servings

The saltiness of prosciutto is a perfect foil for the rich monkfish. This Italian-inspired dish is relatively easy to prepare and very dramatic when plated. Serve it cut into medallions over some cheesy polenta and surround it with the smoked tomato sauce. If you do not have a smoker, you can use an outdoor barbecue. And if this is just too much hassle, you can skip smoking the tomatoes entirely—instead, use a couple of drops of liquid smoke when sautéing the tomatoes and onions. Liquid smoke is available in most grocery stores in a small 7 oz (200 ml) bottle.

Smoked Tomato Sauce

6 very ripe Roma or beefsteak tomatoes

½ cup (100 ml) + ¼ cup (50 ml) extra virgin olive oil

1 large onion, peeled and chopped

1 tsp (5 ml) sugar

salt and pepper, to taste

4 cloves garlic, minced

a pinch of chile flakes

1 cup (200 ml) water

Prosciutto-Wrapped Monkfish

2 filets/tails monkfish (1.2 lb/½ kg each), skin removed and trimmed

salt and pepper, to taste

8 slices prosciutto, very thinly sliced

2 Tbsp (30 ml) extra virgin olive oil

1 cup (250 ml) applewood, hickory, or mesquite chips, or 3 drops liquid smoke

If using wood chips, begin by soaking them in water. To make the sauce: Prepare a smoker or barbecue and smoke the tomatoes for about 20 minutes with fairly heavy smoke. Remove the tomatoes from the smoker and let them cool briefly. Cut tomatoes in half, remove any seeds, and roughly chop them.

In a medium saucepan, heat the ½ cup (100 ml) of olive oil. Add the onion and cook over low heat for 15 minutes. Add the sugar, salt, pepper, and garlic and cook another 5 minutes—do not let the garlic brown. Add the chopped tomatoes, chile flakes, water, and liquid smoke if you have not smoked the tomatoes, and bring to a simmer. Cook 20 minutes, stirring often.

Cool the tomato mixture briefly, remove to a blender, and purée. Be careful when blending hot ingredients—use short pulses at first. Remove the sauce from the blender and strain through a fine sieve. Return the sauce to a saucepan and simmer an additional 5–8 minutes. Whisk in the ¼ cup (50 ml) of olive oil and reserve in a warm place.

Season the monkfish filets with salt and pepper.

Carefully wrap the filets with the prosciutto, taking care to not leave any gaps in the prosciutto wrapping. Wrap the filets tightly in plastic wrap and refrigerate for 15 minutes.

Warm a large non-stick skillet, add the 2 Tbsp (30 ml) of olive oil. Remove the plastic wrap from the filets, taking care to keep the prosciutto on the filets. Place the filets in the pan seam-side down and cook until the prosciutto is browned a bit. Turn the wrapped filets a quarter of the way around and sauté for 3 minutes, repeating for both filets until all sides are lightly browned and a little crispy. With a large spatula, carefully remove the filets to a roasting pan and roast in a 400°F (220°C) oven for about 12 minutes. Remove the filets from the oven and let cool 3 minutes.

Carefully slice the monkfish into thin medallions and serve with the tomato sauce.

ETHICAL EATING NOTE

Please enjoy monkfish sparingly, as there are some significant ethical concerns with eating it. Stocks of monkfish in many countries are significantly depleted. Two challenges to the sustainability of monkfish are that the male fish actually dies in fertilizing the female, and that they can take a very long time to grow. Two very good sustainable substitutes would be farmed catfish or tilapia.

Tandoori Monkfish

Yield ✎ 6 servings

I love this recipe—it captures the spirit of India with a simple rub of spices. Try to avoid using a spice paste or jarred tandoori sauce. Indians traditionally favour a straightforward powdered tandoori spice mix and use it as a rub or mix it with a little yogourt and oil as we do in this recipe. Monkfish filets can vary considerably in weight. For this recipe, it won't matter if one filet is considerably larger or smaller than the other, as the quantities in this recipe are based on the total weight of all monkfish used.

SERVE WITH
raita, basmati rice, and an Indian flatbread like naan

2 filets monkfish (35 oz/1 kg total), cleaned
1 tsp (5 ml) + 1 Tbsp (15 ml) tandoori powder
1 cup (200 ml) full-fat yogourt
¼ cup (50 ml) vegetable oil

Rub the monkfish filets with the 1 tsp (5 ml) of tandoori powder and set aside. In a bowl, combine the 1 Tbsp (15 ml) of tandoori powder, yogourt, and oil, and mix thoroughly. Place the fish in the mixture and marinate for 1–2 hours.

Preheat the oven to 450°F (230°C).

Place a sheet of parchment paper on a sheet tray and place the fish on top of the paper. Place the tray in the oven and roast for 15 minutes. Turn the filets and roast for another 5 minutes. Fish should be firm and a little charred.

Mussels

WHO DOESN'T LOVE MUSSELS? IMAGINE A freshly steamed bowl, overflowing with plump, blue mussels—whether the giant variety or the little tiny ones, which I prefer—a loaf of fresh bread to sop up the cooking juices, and a glass of Muscadet or ice-cold beer.

At the Café Brussels restaurant in Toronto—which my old friend and former chef Ryan Nicholson and I used to visit regularly—they prepared mussels in over fifty different ways, each subtly different.

These sweet treats from the sea benefit from the simplest cooking techniques, although the Spanish Tapas mussel recipe is something that I have long used for canapés at special dinners.

Mussels should be clean, fresh, and smell of the sea. Just before cooking I always rinse them in a couple of changes of fresh, cold water. Most cultivated mussels do not have the "beard" attached like in years past, but if you spot one, just pinch the shell sides together and pull it off. Discard any fresh mussels that do not close when squeezed, that smell "off," or that do not open after they have been cooked.

Iberian Mussels

Yield ⌣ 4 servings

My wife and I really enjoy this recipe at home—the explosion of heat from the chorizo and chile flakes, the hit of garlic that accentuates the mussels, and the sweetish flavour of the sherry wine immediately remind me of seaside tapas bars I visited in Alicante, Spain. Lots of parsley at the end and a final flourish of oil make this an easy treat that will leave you dreaming of the Costa Brava.

SERVE WITH
a Spanish Albarino or a cool fino sherry

¼ cup (50 ml) extra virgin olive oil

1 cup (200 ml) chopped spicy chorizo sausages, about 2 links

4 cloves garlic, minced (more to taste)

½ tsp (2 ml) chile flakes

2 shallots, minced

½ tsp (2 ml) paprika

3.3 lbs (1.5 kg) fresh mussels

1 cup (250 ml) dry sherry

salt and pepper, to taste

1 cup (200 ml) chopped Italian parsley, stems removed

In a large pot that has a tight-fitting lid, warm half of the olive oil over medium heat. Add the chorizo and cook 2–3 minutes or until it is cooked through and starts to brown. Add the garlic, chile flakes, shallots, and paprika. Add the mussels and toss to coat. Add the sherry, salt, and pepper and place the lid on. Increase the heat to high and steam the mussels 5–7 minutes, shaking the pot every minute or so. When done, the mussels should all have opened and smell sweet and salty at the same time. Discard any mussels that have not opened. Add the remaining olive oil and parsley. Toss thoroughly and serve. As an option, you may add a dash of sherry to finish.

Provençale Mussels

Yield ✦ 4 servings

There are many variations on Provençale mussels—some with red wine, some with white, some with cream, and some with tomato. This version speaks to me of the Côte d'Azur, from Marseille to the Italian border, as it is similar to what you can find there at many beach-side cafes.

SERVE WITH

a loaf of fresh crusty bread and a cool glass of Marsanne or a Nova Scotia rosé

¼ cup (50 ml) extra virgin olive oil

1 shallot, minced

6 cloves garlic, minced

3.3 lbs (1.5 kg) fresh mussels

1 cup (200 ml) prepared (or fresh) tomato sauce

1 large ripe tomato, seeded and chopped

salt and pepper, to taste

½ cup (100 ml) black olives, pitted and sliced

1 cup (250 ml) white wine

½ cup (100 ml) chopped fresh basil, stems removed

In a large pot that has a tight-fitting lid, warm half of the olive oil over medium heat. Add the minced shallot and garlic and cook for 1 minute or until the garlic is fragrant. Add the mussels and stir to coat. Add the tomato sauce, tomato, salt, pepper, olives, and wine. Toss quickly then place the lid on the pot, raise the heat to high, and steam the mussels for 5–7 minutes, shaking the pot every minute or so. When done, the mussels should all have opened and smell sweet and salty at the same time. Discard any mussels that have not opened. Add the remaining olive oil and basil, toss a bit, then remove to a large bowl and serve immediately.

Tapas Mussels

Yield ⌒ about 50 canapés

This is a variation on an original recipe by Penelope Casas, Spain's most famous cookbook author, that I have been cooking for fifteen years. A little advance work here will mean only a quick fry at service. A countertop fryer would be very helpful but a pot with oil will suffice too. This is fun to make with friends.

SERVE WITH
a dry sherry

1 Tbsp (15 ml) olive oil

1 shallot, finely chopped

4 cloves garlic, minced

3.3 lbs (1.5 kg) mussels, rinsed

1 cup (200 ml) dry sherry

6 or 7 stalks Italian parsley, stems removed and
    finely chopped

½ cup (100 g) Asiago or manchego cheese,
    grated

1 tsp (5 ml) paprika

½ cup (100 ml) pimento (roasted red pepper,
    peeled), finely chopped.

½ cup (100 ml) bread crumbs

**countertop fryer or medium pot of oil heated
    to 325°F (165°C)**

Béchamel Sauce
1 Tbsp (15 ml) butter
1 Tbsp (15 ml) flour
1 cup (250 ml) milk, warm

In a large pot with a tight-fitting lid, heat the oil, then add the shallot and half of the garlic. Cook one minute or until the garlic is fragrant. Add the mussels and sherry, replace the lid, and steam the mussels for 5–7 minutes or until they are opened. Discard any mussels that do not open. Strain the mussels through a large strainer, reserving the cooking liquids.

Let the mussels cool 10 minutes, then remove the meat from the mussels. Reserve 50 of the shells, cleaning them thoroughly of any beard, tendon, or meat. Dry the shells with a paper towel.

Chop the mussel meat finely. Remove it to a bowl and add the parsley, cheese, remaining garlic, paprika, and pimento. Mix thoroughly, then chill half an hour.

To make the béchamel: In a medium pan, heat the butter until it is foaming, then stir in the flour. Cook for 1–2 minutes, stirring often. Add the milk, reduce the heat to low, and cook until thickened. Add ½ cup (100 ml) of the reserved mussel cooking liquid and stir, and cook 1–2 more minutes, or until thick.

Add half of the béchamel to the mussel mixture and stir to combine. Carefully stuff the half mussel shells with the mussel mixture, packing it in firmly. With a small pastry brush or palette knife, cover the top of the shell with the remaining béchamel, effectively sealing the filling into the shell. Dredge the top of the mussels (the béchamel side) with the bread crumbs. Cover thoroughly and chill the mussels for 1 hour, or until you are ready to serve them.

Heat a fryer to 325°F (165°C) and gently drop the mussels into the oil. Do not overcrowd the mussels. Fry until the bread crumbs are just beginning to turn golden brown, about 2 minutes. Be careful not to overcook the mussels or the filling will melt and fall out. You can test the cooking time with one mussel to start. Repeat until all are cooked. Serve immediately.

Brussels Mussels

Yield ❧ 4 servings

Mussels are a part of Belgian culture and Belgian beer, with its engagingly hoppy, bitter taste, is a great match for mussels. Any good beer will do, but try a Trappist monk beer or a Duvel for a real treat.

1 Tbsp (15 ml) butter
2 cloves garlic, minced
2 shallots, minced
3.3 lbs (1.5 kg) fresh mussels
1 (11 oz/341 ml) bottle of Leffe, Duvel, Stella Artois, or other good-quality beer
1 tsp (5 ml) green peppercorns

In a large pot with a tight-fitting lid, melt the butter over medium heat. Add the garlic and shallots and sauté for 2 minutes, or until the garlic is fragrant. Add the mussels, beer, and peppercorns. Place the lid on the pot and steam the mussels for 5–7 minutes or until they have all opened. Shake the pot occasionally to move the mussels. Discard any mussels that have not opened, and serve immediately.

Oysters

IT IS SAID THAT AMERICAN BUSINESSMAN Diamond Jim Brady regularly ate one hundred oysters at a sitting. The passion that many bring to the consumption of this minute bivalve is unmatched when compared to other seafood.

The oyster evokes passion. Long associated with virility and stamina, oysters are featured on menus regularly around anniversaries, Valentine's Day, and birthdays. Raw or cooked, oysters are a definitive statement that much from the sea is delicious.

Oysters on the Half Shell with Kiwi Mignonette

Yield ⌒ 12 servings

I love the refreshing and often mouth-clanging tartness of kiwi with the rich (sometimes metallic) briny blast of freshly shucked oysters. Kiwis are guilty of a hefty carbon footprint, considering how far they have travelled to get here, so it is hard to consider using them with so many other wonderful products from our own backyard. However, several years ago, I learned that an intrepid grower, Mike Hanson, has been growing a variety called the Arctic kiwi, or hardy kiwi, in Nova Scotia (not 20 km from our restaurant) for a number of years. Smaller in size than a typical kiwi, it is about the size of an aggie marble and its flesh is more yellow than a New Zealand kiwi. Originally native to China, Arctic kiwis have been found to flourish in cold climates where regular kiwis do not grow at all.

SERVE WITH
Champagne or a good quality sparkling white

  9 ripe Arctic kiwis or 3 ripe kiwis
  ½ tsp (2 ml) sugar
  2 Tbsp (30 ml) rice wine vinegar
  ½ inch (1 cm) ginger, peeled and minced
  1 clove garlic, finely minced
  1 shallot, peeled and finely minced
  Tabasco, to taste
  36–48 oysters, depending upon the hunger of
    your guests

Peel the kiwis and dice into very small cubes. Dissolve the sugar in the rice wine vinegar. Combine all the ingredients except for the oysters. Wash the oysters to remove any surface dirt or mud and shuck them carefully. Top each shucked oyster with a small dollop of the kiwi mignonette and enjoy immediately.

TECHNIQUE TIDBIT
Shucking Oysters: I have opened thousands of oysters. When I first was a server at the Red Snapper on King Street in Toronto (in the mid-1980s), I shucked more than one hundred per night. I worked there for five days a week for thirteen months—you do the math. You need a strong arm, and a good oyster knife with a thumb guard, especially if you need to shuck a lot. Always clean oysters thoroughly under cold, fresh running water before shucking them to cut down on any potential grit—to my mind the only sullying factor in the consumption of shellfish is the occasional unfortunate mouthful of grit or sand from an unrinsed specimen.

I always have a kitchen towel in hand when opening oysters—I find it helps the process go more quickly as you can hold an oyster more firmly and with less danger of stabbing yourself.

Oyster and Tomato Water Shooters

Yield ☙ 12 shooters

This is fun food for a summertime or early fall alfresco party. A tray of these, passed around a convivial gathering, is sure to engender conversation and perhaps later, l'amour! Find a dollar store and buy twelve inexpensive shooter glasses or jiggers and keep them for this recipe. You will pull this one out a lot, I bet.

6 very ripe tomatoes

2 stalks celery, chopped

1 medium onion, peeled and chopped

3 cloves garlic, peeled and roughly chopped

1 tsp (5 ml) salt + salt, to taste

ground black pepper, to taste

1 Tbsp (15 ml) prepared horseradish, or 1 tsp (5 ml) fresh grated horseradish

12 oysters, cleaned

1 tsp (5 ml) chopped chives, or green onions, sliced very thin

cheesecloth

The day before, combine the tomatoes, celery, onion, garlic, salt, pepper, and horseradish in the bowl of a food processor. (Do this in batches if your processor is small.) Blend until a chunky mass forms, about one minute.

Line a large colander or strainer with the cheesecloth and place over a bowl that will catch the strained liquid. Carefully pour the tomato pulp into the strainer. Place the strainer/bowl assembly in the fridge for 6–8 hours or overnight, and allow it to drain. The next morning, discard the solids and retain the clear liquid. There should be 2 cups (500 ml) or so. Add salt to taste.

Right before serving, shuck the cleaned oysters and pour them into a small strainer placed over a small bowl to catch the oyster liquid. Take care to ensure there are no oyster shell bits or dirt particles among the oysters. Place a shucked oyster in each of the shot glasses. Divide the oyster liquid among the shot glasses and then top with the reserved tomato water. Top each glass with chives or green onions. Serve immediately.

Crispy Cornmeal-Battered Oysters with Spicy Remoulade

Yield ☙ 4 appetizer servings

My wife loves oysters in their purest form—raw on the half shell—but she guiltily admitted to really enjoying this cooked version the first time I made them at Tempest. Perhaps her southern roots are showing through (she was born in Tennessee). I love the food of Louisiana, and you can find variations on this recipe in hundreds of New Orleans restaurants, where oyster po' boys are made with deep-fried oysters served on soft, squishy buns. Here, the oysters are fried only a minute—so that the outsides are crunchy but the inside are still soft, moist, and barely cooked—served on top of a spicy remoulade, and put back in the half shell.

Remoulade

½ cup (100 ml) mayonnaise
2 Tbsp (30 ml) white wine vinegar
Tabasco, to taste
Worcestershire sauce, to taste
1 Tbsp (15 ml) grainy Dijon mustard
1 tsp (5 ml) capers, chopped
6 green olives, pitted and finely minced
1 stalk celery, finely minced
1 Tbsp (15 ml) Italian parsley, finely chopped
¼ tsp (1 ml) paprika
salt and pepper, to taste

Cornmeal-Battered Oysters

16 large oysters, cleaned
1 cup (200 ml) fine cornmeal
salt and pepper, to taste

countertop fryer or large pot of oil heated to
350°F (180°C)

Combine the remoulade ingredients in a small bowl and let the flavours meld for 1–2 hours in the fridge.

Shuck the oysters carefully and place the shucked meat on a plate lined with several layers of paper towel. Clean, dry, and reserve the shells. Place the shells on a serving tray and divide the remoulade among them.

Dry the oysters thoroughly. Heat some vegetable or canola oil to 350°F (180°C) in a large deep pan (or a countertop deep-fryer). Dredge the oysters thoroughly in the cornmeal and then deep-fry for 1 minute, or until the cornmeal is crunchy. Remove the oysters to a tray lined with paper towel to absorb the excess oil. Season the oysters with salt, and pepper and place 1 fried oyster in each shell on the remoulade sauce. Serve immediately.

Salmon

SALMON—HIGH IN HEALTHY ESSENTIAL OILS
and omega-3 fatty acids—has been prized by many chefs
as the king of fish. With its unparalleled taste and firm
texture well-suited to a variety of cooking methods, it is
one of the most versatile seafoods.

One of the best ways to purchase salmon is to buy a
whole side, usually around four pounds (two kilograms).
It is often cheaper this way and if you purchase it fresh,
you can cut it easily and freeze individual portions for
later use. Remove the skin if desired, but there is plenty of
nutrition packed in there if you wish to keep it and cook
with it on. Portion the fish carefully into six-ounce (two
-hundred-gram) pieces, wrap it in plastic or vacuum pack
it, and freeze. For a four-pound (two-kilogram) side, you
should be able to get ten to twelve equal-sized portions,
but cut them according to how healthy your appetite is.
Retain extra trim pieces for use in a quick salmon chowder
or in the Sole Stuffed with Smoked Salmon Mousse
(page 104).

Yucca-Crusted Salmon with Pirri Pirri Sauce

Yield ☙ 6 servings

I love salmon many ways, but particularly with a crispy crust. One of my favourite methods of preparing salmon is to crust it with grated yucca (also called cassava or manioc). When cooked on the surface of the fish, it gets beautifully crispy and retains moisture. Buy a hunk of yucca and cut off only what you need for this recipe, about ½ lb (150–200 g). Peel it with a sharp knife and then grate it on the large holes of a box grater. Use it immediately. The rest of the yucca will fry up nicely as chips! Pirri Pirri sauce is a spicy South American sauce equally good on beef or fish. Make this several days ahead to allow the flavours to commingle. It will keep well in the fridge, sealed, for two weeks. Salmon steak, halibut, grouper, wahoo, or kingfish can be substituted for the filet.

SERVE OVER
rice pilaf made with pumpkin seeds

Pirri Pirri Sauce

2 cups (500 ml) extra virgin olive oil

2 whole poblano chiles, roasted, peeled, and seeded

2 jalapeno peppers, chopped and stems removed (keep seeds)✱

1 tsp (5 ml) red chile flakes

1 tsp (5 ml) salt

1 tsp (5 ml) ground black pepper

1 Tbsp (15 ml) minced garlic, about 3 cloves

4 sprigs cilantro, washed and chopped, stem ends removed

✱ **Use rubber gloves to keep the spicy heat of the seeds from getting on your skin.**

Yucca-Crusted Salmon

6 portions salmon filet (½ lb/200 g each)

salt and pepper, to taste

1 cup (200 ml) peeled and grated yucca (avoid the stringy core)

2 Tbsp (30 ml) olive or grapeseed oil

ETHICAL EATING NOTE

There are two distinct camps regarding farmed salmon. Aqua-culturists can produce much evidence that farmed salmon is healthy and does not harm the environment. Activists and naturalists, however, have their own evidence that penned animals swimming in a confined area can cause contamination. While significant improvements are being made in the field of salmon farming management, I personally choose not to serve salmon at Tempest, and substitute sea trout or Arctic char. If you are lucky enough to live where wild salmon are still viable and available (like Alaska) I would encourage you to try some. We used to get Alaskan Copper River salmon flown to us in Chicago, and it was a rare and glorious treat.

To prepare the Pirri Pirri Sauce, combine the olive oil, chile peppers, chile flakes, salt, and black pepper in a saucepan. Bring the liquid to a boil and reduce the heat. Simmer the sauce for 4 minutes and remove from heat.

Stir in the garlic and cilantro. With a hand-held mixer, or carefully using a blender, purée the sauce until smooth. Refrigerate the sauce for at least one day before serving. The sauce can be served at room temperature.

To prepare the salmon, begin by seasoning the fish with salt and pepper. Pack a thin layer of the grated yucca directly onto one side of the fish. Press down solidly so that it stays adhered.

Preheat the oven to 400°F (200°C).

Heat a large non-stick skillet over medium heat. Add the oil and carefully place the fish in the pan yucca side down. Sauté over medium heat, without moving or touching the fish, until a solid crust forms and there are brown bits along the visible edges of the salmon, about 4 minutes. The crust should have the appearance of hash browns. Using a fish flipper, carefully flip the fish over and cook another 2 minutes. Remove to a sheet tray and place in a hot oven for 3 minutes, or until cooked to your liking.

Remove from the oven and serve with the Pirri Pirri Sauce.

Medallions of Salmon with Sauerkraut and Black Trumpet Mushrooms

Yield ❧ 6–8 servings

This was a signature dish at The Everest Room—I literally made it thousands of times. I recreate it here as it has been part of my repertoire since I was a young chef, but also as homage to my mentor, Everest Chef Jean Joho. This is a complicated dish, best for foodies, but if you are game to try, the results are rewarding.

SERVE WITH
a favourite starch

3.5 oz (100 g) fresh black trumpet mushrooms, or 1.8 oz (25 g) dried mushrooms, reconstituted in hot water for half an hour

1 Tbsp (15 ml) butter

1 shallot, peeled and minced

2 cloves garlic, minced

½ cup (100 ml) fruity white wine like Alsace Gewürztraminer

1 salmon side (3.3 lbs/1.5 kg), skin off, trimmed of any brown belly fat

salt and pepper, to taste

1 cup (200 g) sauerkraut, drained of excess liquid

1 Tbsp (15 ml) fresh chives, thinly sliced

olive or grapeseed oil, for sautéing

1 roll stretchy cling film

Chive Vin Blanc Sauce

1 Tbsp (15 ml) butter + 1 cup (200 g) chilled unsalted butter, cubed

1 shallot, minced

6 black peppercorns

3 sprigs fresh thyme

1 clove garlic, minced

1 cup (250 ml) dry white wine

¼ cup (50 ml) heavy whipping cream

salt and Tabasco, to taste

To prepare the Chive Vin Blanc Sauce, heat the 1 Tbsp (15 ml) butter in a medium saucepan. Add the shallot and peppercorns and sweat 5 minutes. Add the thyme and garlic and cook 1 more minute. Add the wine, stir, and reduce by half (about 5 minutes). Add the cream and bring back to a boil. With a whisk, incorporate the 1 cup (200 g) of butter while whisking in a cube at a time. Keep the mixture just on the edge of a boil. Add the butter evenly and slowly (over 4 minutes). When done, pour the sauce through a strainer into another small saucepan to remove the thyme, shallot, and peppercorns. Season with salt and Tabasco and keep in a warm place until ready to serve.

Now prepare the mushrooms. If using dried mushrooms, drain them from the soaking liquid. Melt the butter in a sauté pan over medium heat. Add the mushrooms and shallot and sweat for 8–10 minutes. Add the garlic and cook 2 more minutes. Deglaze with the white wine and cook until the liquid has evaporated, about 4 minutes. Remove from the pan and allow to cool.

The biggest trick of this recipe is properly cutting the filet. With the whole filet in front of you on a cutting board, cut it in half lengthwise, then cut widthwise across the final third of the filet (see diagram next page) creating 4 pieces—2 large, vaguely rectangular pieces and 2 elongated triangles formed by the tail end.

Roll out a large piece of cling film in front of you. Keep it attached to the roll so that you can continue to roll out more around the fish.

Take the largest piece of the filet, the top section, and lay it on top of the cling film with the former skin side facing you, and the thickest part of the filet at the top. Season with salt and pepper, then press half of the sauerkraut onto the surface. Cover with a thin line of the cooled mushrooms. Cover

Preparing your filet

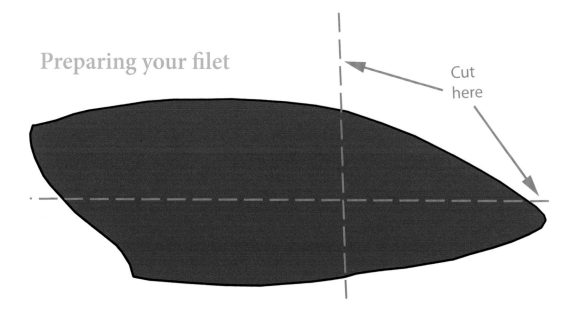

Cut here

the mushrooms with the remaining sauerkraut. Carefully lay the second-largest piece of salmon filet against the first piece, and then cover the remaining area with the 2 triangular pieces. Essentially you are encapsulating the filling inside the pieces of filet.

Roll the "roulade" in the cling film, occasionally tucking in the ends of the film to create a tight roll about 2 inches (5 cm) in diameter. Use about a metre of cling film. Refrigerate for one hour before cooking.

When ready to cook, use a very sharp knife and cut the salmon roll into medallions about ½ inch (2 cm) thick, leaving the plastic wrap on the medallions. Heat a large non-stick frying pan over medium heat and add some olive oil or grapeseed oil. Place the medallions, plastic and all, in the pan and sauté until golden on the first side, about 2 minutes. Carefully flip over and cook the other side 2 more minutes.

Remove the medallions to a cutting board and let them cool briefly before carefully removing the plastic wrap (I hold down the medallion with a fish flipper and use needlenose pliers to grab one edge of the plastic, pulling it up and off the medallion). Place the medallions on a tray in a hot oven for 2 minutes while you reheat the Chive Vin Blanc Sauce on the stove over medium heat. Do not boil the sauce. Pour the sauce on each serving plate and then top with 2 or 3 medallions per person.

Salt Cod

FOR HUNDREDS OF YEARS, SALT COD WAS A staple of both the North American and European diet. Stories from the past tell of cod so abundant that one was able to virtually walk on water off the coast of Newfoundland for the surfeit of cod in the sea below.

Sadly, overfishing by the factory trawlers of many nations have virtually wiped out cod stocks—not just in the North Atlantic, but worldwide. Amongst the most voracious fishing nations are Spain and Portugal, whose factory ships have plied all of the earth's oceans in search of cod, the basis of their beloved *bacalhau*. Most of the salt cod available now is actually salted lingcod—also called bluefish or blue cod—which is still in relatively good supply although the meat is not as sweet as true Atlantic cod.

Salt Cod Croquettes

Yield ∾ about 36 croquettes

This easy Spanish tapas is great finger food for a party. Start to soak the salt cod or salt fish several days ahead if you can, and change the water a couple of times to ensure that the fish is not too salty. This goes well with the Smoked Tomato Sauce (page 54).

2 lbs (1 kg) salt fish, soaked overnight
1 Tbsp (15 ml) shallots, finely diced
2 cups (500 ml) mashed potatoes
1 egg, beaten + 3 eggs, lightly beaten
1 cup (200 ml) flour
1 cup (200 ml) bread crumbs

countertop fryer or large pot of oil heated to
   350°F (180°C)

Simmer the fish and shallots together in lots of water over medium heat until the fish is flaky (about 15 minutes). Strain and cool. Break apart and flake the fish.

Mix the fish with the mashed potato and the first beaten egg. Chill for 1 hour. Form the mixture into croquettes (small cylinders around ½ inch/1 cm wide and 1 ½ inch/3 cm long). Roll each croquette in flour, dip it into the remaining eggs, and then roll it in the bread crumbs. Chill again for 1 hour.

Preheat a fryer or pot of vegetable oil to 350°F (180°C) and fry the croquettes until golden brown, about 4 minutes. Drain on paper towel before serving. Serve with Smoked Tomato Sauce (page 58).

Esqueixada (Shredded Salt Cod Salad)

Yield ☙ 6 servings

Salt pollock would be an acceptable substitute in this Catalan dish we have served at Tempest. The fish in this recipe is not cooked, so the cod must be soaked for at least 48 hours. It's essential to find the best ingredients, especially ripe tomatoes and a really fruity, preferably Spanish, olive oil.

1.10 lbs (500 g) salt cod, or salt pollock

½ cup (125 ml) milk

1 onion, sliced paper thin and separated in rings

½ green bell pepper, seeded and finely diced

½ red bell pepper, seeded and finely diced

2 tomatoes, seeded and chopped

2 Tbsp (30 ml) extra virgin olive oil, or more for consistency

balsamic vinegar, to taste

salt and ground black pepper, to taste

1 cup (500 ml) green olives

Cover the salt cod with water and place it in the refrigerator for 48 hours, changing the water at least 3 times. Add the milk to the last change of water. Then, when ready to begin preparations, carefully drain off all the liquid, remove any skin or bones, and finely shred the fish with your fingers.

Combine the salt cod, onion, peppers, and tomatoes in a salad bowl and mix well. Dress with the oil and vinegar, then marinate for at least 24 hours or more, covered, in a non-metallic container in the refrigerator. Before serving, add black pepper, and if necessary, salt to taste. Garnish with olives and serve.

Scallops

Scallops are synonymous with Nova Scotia. Whether deep-fried in a crunchy batter, wrapped in some smoky bacon and baked, or seared till crispy in a cast iron skillet and served with a creamy sauce, they represent traditional Maritime eating at its finest.

Scallops are very adaptable to a great number of preparations. I am including a couple of non-traditional ones here for you to flesh out your scallop repertoire.

Seared Scallops with Chive Vin Blanc Sauce

Yield ⌒ 6 servings

This has been on the Tempest menu for years with the delicious beauties from scallop farmer Peter Darnell front and centre. Be sure to keep the shells if you can and use them to present the dish. At the restaurant we often serve the scallops with the roe on for both dramatic effect and subtle briny flavour.

36 fresh scallops
1 Tbsp (15 ml) extra virgin olive oil,
   for drizzling
salt and pepper, to taste
½ cup (100 g) fresh seaweed, washed (or
   seaweed salad)
1 Tbsp (15 ml) butter
1 recipe Chive Vin Blanc Sauce (page 72)
6 chives, finely chopped

Shuck the scallops. If desired, try to leave the roe attached and remove all other entrails. Wash them if necessary, but dry again with a towel. Drizzle the scallops with a little olive oil and season with salt and pepper. Let the scallops sit for 15 minutes while you make the sauce. Reserve the scallop shells to serve, but make sure to clean them thoroughly.

Put the seaweed on the serving plates. Place the reserved shells on top of the seaweed.

Sear the scallops in the butter in a hot pan until they are golden brown on one side only, about 4 minutes. Remove and place a scallop on top of each shell. Quickly re-warm the chive sauce—do not boil it—and toss in the chives. Stir to incorporate, pour over the scallops, and serve.

ETHICAL EATING NOTE

Digby scallops, known the world over as a quintessential Nova Scotia food, are delicious, but there have long been issues with dredging the sea bottom to harvest them. Typically this results in an abundant harvest, and recent evidence suggests that scallops actually thrive in post-dredged waters, but there is empirical evidence to suggest that entire aquatic habitats that other creatures call home are irrevocably harmed by this practice. At our restaurant, we serve hand-harvested, farmed scallops that are line-hung in the sea and act as living water purifiers, with minimal damage done to the sea bottom. They are smaller than the monsters we see at many restaurants as a main course, but I feel they are sweeter. My supplier, Indian Point Marine Farms, often has these scallops for sale at the Halifax Farmers' Market. In New England, look for diver scallops whenever possible. These grow in the wild, but are hand-harvested by a scuba diver and thus do not disturb the marine habitat.

Scallop, Mango, and Passion Fruit Seviche

Yield ✑ 6 servings

Seviche, described at the beginning of this book, is a classic Latin American method of preparing seafood, where it is "cooked" in citrus. This dish is perfectly suited to a picnic on a beach or boat. Serve in a clear glass for dramatic effect.

SERVE WITH
plantain chips

36 small bay scallops, shucked and cleaned
¼ cup (60 ml) sliced red onion
1 mango, peeled, seeded, and cut into ½-inch
   (1-cm) cubes
1 pint (400 g) ripe cherry tomatoes
1 small jalapeno pepper, seeded, and minced
4 stalks green onion, sliced on a bias
1 tsp (5 ml) fresh minced ginger
2 Tbsp (30 ml) passion fruit purée, or the pulp
   of 2 fresh passion fruits
¼ cup (60 ml) extra virgin olive oil
sugar, to taste
salt and pepper, to taste
1 large lime
12 sprigs fresh cilantro

Combine all ingredients except the lime and cilantro in a large non-metallic bowl. If scallops are large, cut them in half.

Wash and dry the lime. With a microplane zester or fine grater, grate the lime zest over the seviche. Cut the lime in half and squeeze the juice on. Toss the seviche thoroughly and marinate for 1 hour.

Roughly chop half of the cilantro and stir it into seviche. Divide the mixture among 6 glasses and garnish each glass with a sprig of cilantro or plantain chip.

Yucatan Scallops with Avocado Salsa

Yield ☙ 6 servings

Achiote Powder, made from annatto seeds, is what gives the scallops the distinctive red colour and superb flavour in this very easy recipe. It can be found in packets at most Latin American markets. The salsa is really just a chunky guacamole—you know, Super Bowl food for scallops! This dish is best made with larger scallops. Ask your fishmonger for U30 scallops, which means about 30 scallops per pound.

36 scallops (1.1 lbs/500 g total)
1 (0.3 oz/10 g) packet achiote powder
1 Tbsp (15 ml) olive oil
1 bowl Avocado Salsa (page 17)
fresh cilantro, for garnish

Carefully remove any adductor tissue (the little firm piece of flesh on the side of the scallops) from the scallops. Place the scallops in a bowl. Open the packet of achiote powder and sprinkle it over the scallops. Add half of the olive oil and toss to coat the scallops thoroughly. Let the scallops marinate in the fridge for 1 hour, stirring occasionally.

Add the other half of the olive oil to a medium-hot pan or spray cooking oil onto a hot grill and add the scallops. Cook the scallops on one side for 3 minutes, then flip and cook another 2 minutes—do not overcook. Scallops can be eaten raw and in this recipe are best served medium-rare. Divide the salsa among the plates and top with 6 scallops per portion. Garnish each with a sprig of fresh cilantro.

Shrimp

WHO DOESN'T LOVE SHRIMP? ENJOYED BY virtually every culture on earth, shrimp are succulent, sweet, and fun to eat. I have a fond memory of eating shrimp in Greece with my wife in February 1991. On the advice of a *Rough Guide* guidebook, we were in the seaside town of Haraki on the southeastern coast of the island of Rhodes in the Aegean Sea—a nowhereville resort village. The day was sunny but not particularly warm for Greece (about 66°F/ 18°C). Most of the town's restaurants and hotels were shut tight for the winter, but the locals were lined up on the promenade, watching a parade and partying as part of a local festival.

Just outside of the town, the guidebook said, was Efterpi, a most amazing beachside grill where the proprietor was famous for colossal fresh prawns. Purportedly, the prawns were locally caught and grilled over an open flame in a little local olive oil and lemon with some fresh herbs thrown right on the fire to perfume and smoke. We were the only customers that day and true enough, the prawns were the biggest I had ever seen, each about the size of a lobster (I swear!). They were moist, sweet, and delectable! I also remember that half a kilo of them were almost forty dollars, but worth every drachma!

Coconut-Crusted Jumbo Shrimp Cocktail

Yield ✐ 6 servings

This is an easy appetizer that turns elegant when served in a martini glass. The shrimp can be baked or fried.

12 jumbo shrimp, peeled and deveined
¼ cup (50 ml) bread crumbs
⅔ cup (150 ml) flaked, dried coconut (not
    sweetened)
1 cup (200 ml) flour
2 eggs, lightly beaten

12 (6-inch/15 cm) skewers
countertop fryer or large pot of oil heated to
    350°F (180°C) or vegetable oil for spraying
    and baking

Cocktail Sauce
1 cup (200 ml) tomato ketchup
1 ripe mango, peeled, seeded, and roughly
    chopped
1 Tbsp (15 ml) horseradish
1 tsp (5 ml) Worcestershire sauce
2 Tbsp (30 ml) orange juice
1 small onion, peeled and chopped
½ cup (100 ml) water

Place all cocktail sauce ingredients in a food processor and purée for 2 minutes, or until smooth. Divide equally among 6 martini glasses.

To prepare the shrimp, attach one to each skewer by holding them as straight as possible in one hand and skewering all the way through, starting at the tail end. Leave each shrimp on the end of each skewer—imagine a Popsicle stick.

Combine the bread crumbs and coconut in a flat pan. Roll each shrimp in the flour and shake off any excess. Dip in the egg and then dredge in the coconut/bread crumb mixture. Reserve on a tray.

To cook, heat a fryer or deep pan with vegetable oil to 350°F (180°C) and deep-fry the shrimp until golden brown, about 4 minutes. Alternatively, spray the shrimps with cooking oil and place them in a hot (450°F/ 230°C) oven and bake for 7–8 minutes, or until golden brown. Serve hot.

Place the shrimps in the martini glass with the shrimp end facing down for easy handling.

ETHICAL EATING NOTE

Most of the world's supply of shrimp is actually raised in tidal pools in Bangladesh, Thailand, India, and some South American countries like Ecuador. The method of farming is an environmental nightmare. The recent tsunami in Bangladesh in 2004 would not have had such a devastating effect if most of the coastline had not been deforested to create these gigantic shrimp farms.

Try to search out trap-caught shrimp or wild shrimp. They may be a little smaller than the monster prawns, but you can be guaranteed that your enjoyment of them has a more modest impact on our environment. Adjust cooking times down if shrimp are smaller than recipes indicate.

Kataifi-Wrapped Shrimp with Sweet Sour Sauce

Yield ∽ 6 servings

This dish makes repeated visits to our menu and is a big hit whenever we offer it. Dramatic plate presentation and great crunchy texture make this a crowd pleaser. Kataifi is simply shredded filo dough. It is available at virtually all Middle Eastern markets in the freezer section. Sambal olek is a spicy garlic chile sauce available in Asian markets. A countertop fryer is the best tool for cooking this dish.

SERVE WITH
a refreshing coleslaw and mashed potato
or yucca

24 jumbo shrimp, peeled and deveined
salt and pepper, to taste
½ cup (100 ml) flour
1 egg, lightly beaten
¼ cup (50 ml) water
1 box kataifi, thawed

countertop fryer or large pot of oil heated to
    350°F (180°C)
24 (6-inch/15 cm) wooden skewers

Sweet Sour Sauce
1 cup (250 ml) ketchup
½ cup (100 ml) pineapple juice
¼ cup (50 ml) rice wine vinegar
¼ cup (50 ml) dry sherry
1 tsp (5 ml) sambal olek
2 Tbsp (30 ml) honey
1 Tbsp (15 ml) soy sauce
1 tsp (5 ml) cornstarch mixed with
    ¼ cup (50 ml) water

Starting at the tails, straighten the shrimp as best you can and skewer them each onto a skewer. Season with salt and pepper and set aside.

Mix the flour, egg, and water in a bowl until smooth. It should be the texture of pancake batter. Refrigerate for 10 minutes. Take the kataifi out of its plastic wrapper and pull it apart gently. (You will not require all of the kataifi for this recipe, but you can refreeze the rest.)

For each shrimp, lay out a rectangle of kataifi about the width of the shrimp and 4 inches (10 cm) long. Dip each shrimp in the batter and drain off any excess. Roll the shrimp along the rectangle of kataifi so that the batter helps it adhere completely around the shrimp. Place in a single layer on a sheet tray while you repeat with the remaining shrimp. When all are done, refrigerate.

For the sauce, add all the ingredients to a medium saucepan and bring to a low boil. Skim any scum that rises to the surface with a small ladle. Stir regularly to avoid scorching. Cook about 10 minutes, then cool. Thin out with a little water if necessary.

To serve, preheat the fryer or pot of vegetable or canola oil to 350°F (180°C) and fry the shrimp a couple at a time for 3–4 minutes. As the shrimp are placed in the oil, spin them a little to keep the

kataifi wrapped around them. Do not overcrowd the shrimp in the oil. Drain on paper towel and season with salt. Keep in a warm oven while you complete the remaining shrimp.

To serve, place 4 shrimp in each serving bowl and drizzle each serving with sauce.

Shrimp Tagliatelle with Pernod Cream, Broccoli, and Feta

Yield ❧ 4 servings

Shrimp, pasta, and cream seem to be made for one another, and I love the flavour of anise with shrimp. This easy dish is great for a quick Friday dinner after a long day. It can be made in twenty minutes. Buy frozen shrimp that have already been cooked and peeled for this dish. To keep the dish low in fat, you can exchange the cream for some low- or non-fat yogourt, but do not boil it. You can use any long pasta, such as fettuccine, linguini, or tagliatelle. Cooked broccoli is in the recipe, but you can substitute green beans, peas, spinach, or leftovers from yesterday's dinner to make this a really quick meal.

1 (18 oz/500 g) box dried tagliatelle

1 Tbsp (15 ml) olive oil

½ cup (100 ml) white wine

1 Tbsp (20 ml) Pernod, ouzo, or sambuca

1 cup (200 ml) heavy cream or low-fat yogurt

14 oz (400 g) cooked shrimp, peeled and
   deveined

14 oz (400 g) broccoli crowns, cooked

1 cup (200 g) feta cheese, crumbled into
   chunks

Cook the pasta according to package directions—keep al dente. Drain the pasta, toss it with olive oil to keep it from sticking, and reserve.

Pour the wine in a large skillet and bring to a simmer. Add the Pernod and bring to a boil. Add the cream and cook for 5 minutes, or until thickened a little. (If using yogourt, bring to a simmer.) When the cream has thickened or the yogourt is just beginning to simmer, immediately add the shrimp, broccoli, and pasta, and toss for 1 minute, or until everything is hot. Divide the pasta evenly among 4 bowls, top with crumbled feta, and serve.

Shrimp, Avocado, and Papaya Towers

Yield ☙ 6 servings

This terrific tropical appetizer will make you pine for a quick trip to Key West or St. Barts. It can be made earlier in the day and plated just before serving. I use a two-inch ring mould to plate it, but you could easily cut the top and bottom off a small tomato paste can and use it instead. Warm Mango Coulis (page 16) or Roasted Red Pepper Aioli (page 39), that has been thinned with a little water, are suitable and colourful sauces to punch up the look and flavour of the dish.

1.10 lbs (500 g) medium shrimp, cooked, shells and tails removed, deveined
1 small ripe papaya, peeled, seeded, and cut in ½-inch (1-cm) cubes
1 ripe avocado, peeled, seed removed, and cut in ½-inch (1-cm) cubes
1 tsp (5 ml) lemon juice
1 Tbsp (15 ml) mayonnaise
1 Tbsp (15 ml) extra virgin olive oil
1 clove garlic, minced
1 tsp (5 ml) fresh ginger, peeled and minced
4 stalks green onion, chopped
2 sprigs fresh cilantro, chopped, for garnish

Chop the cleaned shrimp into ¼-inch (½-cm) pieces. In a bowl large enough to hold everything, combine all the ingredients and toss gently. Allow the flavours to meld for 1 hour.

Divide the mixture among 6 plates and tamp it carefully into a 2-inch ring mould that is 2 inches high. If desired, garnish them with cilantro leaves and surround the towers with the sauce of your choice.

Smoked Seafood

SMOKED SEAFOOD HAS BEEN PART OF Maritime culture since time immemorial. Native Canadians and Americans preserved their seafood catches this way, smoking them with maple or cedar. European culture has been enjoying smoked fish since the halcyon days of ancient Greece and Rome.

This flavour enhancer is a welcome change from other methods of preparing seafood. Most smoked seafood needs no further cooking and can be enjoyed as is. Check the packaging information on whatever products you purchase to ensure that they do not require further cooking.

Smoked Haddock (*Finnan Haddie*)

Yield ☙ 8 servings

This is a classic French treatment of an age-old Maritime dish. Traditionally, the fish and potatoes are combined and baked, casserole-style. In this deconstructed version, smoked haddock is steeped in a creamy broth redolent with fresh thyme, shallots, and peppercorn and poached until it is tender and flakes to the touch. Lovely organic fingerling potatoes cooked in a rich cream sauce lie underneath the fish, just waiting to be discovered. Fingerling potatoes can be bought organically and locally at many farmer's markets and farm stands. Even large supermarkets now carry fingerlings.

30 small fingerling potatoes or (2.2 lbs/1 kg)
    new potatoes
2.2 lbs (1 kg) smoked haddock or cod
1 tsp (5 ml) butter
2 shallots, peeled and cut in rings
12 black or green peppercorns
1 cup (200 ml) white wine
4 sprigs fresh thyme
1 cup (200 ml) fish stock or water
1 cup (200 ml) heavy cream (35%)
1 recipe Chive Vin Blanc Sauce (page 80)

Boil the potatoes in well-salted water until they are tender, about 20 minutes on a medium boil. Drain, cool briefly, and, with a paring knife, carefully peel.

Slice the potatoes into ¼-inch (½-cm) medallions, cutting carefully across the width of the potatoes. Reserve the sliced potatoes.

With a sharp knife, carefully trim the smoked fish of as much silver skin and tough, thin outer edges as possible. Check that there are no pin/fin bones and remove any by cutting them out. Cut the trimmed filets into 8 equal-sized pieces. Reserve.

In a large pot that can hold a minimum of 16 cups (4 litres), melt the butter over medium heat. Add the shallots and peppercorns and cook gently for 2–3 minutes. Add the wine, thyme, stock or water, cream, and any extra bits of the fish trim that can be removed from the broth later. Bring this mixture to a simmer and cook over low heat for 5 minutes.

Place the trimmed smoked fish pieces in the steaming broth and poach on low heat for 15 minutes, or until the fish flakes easily. Meanwhile, prepare the Chive Vin Blanc Sauce. While it is still warm, place the sliced fingerling potatoes in it to reheat. Should

the sauce require any thinning at this stage, add some of the fish-poaching broth after straining it through a fine strainer.

When the fish is cooked and flaky and the pieces are just hanging together, they are done. Place a scoop of the potatoes on the bottom of a small plate.

Make sure there is a generous amount of the strained sauce on the plate as well. Using a fish flipper, flat metal spatula, or slotted spoon, place a piece of fish on top of the potato mixture. Ladle a little more of the cooking broth over the fish and serve.

Finnan Haddie and Chorizo Chowder

Yield ☙ 12 servings

Finnan Haddie references an old Maritime casserole that was typically made of smoked haddock or cod cooked with butter, milk, and potatoes. This chowder is a signature dish at Tempest, a non-traditional spin on an age-old favourite. Here, smoked fish replaces fresh fish and spicy Spanish-style pork and paprika sausage replaces the more traditional bacon. Smoked cod could replace the haddock if necessary.

3 Tbsp (45 ml) olive oil

4 links chorizo sausage (1 ⅓ lbs/550 g total), casings removed

1 large carrot, diced

1 large white onion, diced

2 stalks celery, diced

3 cloves fresh garlic, minced

3 large white potatoes, peeled and diced

¼ tsp (1 ml) chile flakes

3 (8 oz/250 ml) cans of whole evaporated milk

4 cups (1 litre) smoked fish stock, regular fish stock, or water

4 bay leaves

Tabasco, to taste

2 filets line-caught smoked haddock (2 lbs/900 g total)

salt and pepper, to taste

In a large soup pot, heat the oil over medium heat. Add the sausage casings and cook for 10 minutes, stirring to break the pieces up into small bits. When mostly cooked but not crispy, add the carrot, onion, and celery and continue cooking for 10 minutes. Add the garlic, potatoes, chile flakes, evaporated milk, stock or water, bay leaves, and Tabasco and bring to a simmer, stirring the bottom of pan to keep the ingredients from sticking.

Reduce heat to low and cook for 10 minutes or until potatoes are mostly cooked.

Trim the fish of silver skin, cut out any bones, and cut the fish into chunks. Reserve the trimmings for making fish stock later.

Add the fish to the pot and cook gently until the fish flakes, about 10 minutes. Stir often to avoid scorching. Add salt and pepper, to taste. Best enjoyed the next day when reheated so that the flavours are infused.

TECHNIQUE TIDBIT

The trimmings of smoked haddock can make an excellent smoked fish stock. When you purchase smoked haddock, trim away any silver skin, bones, or dried up end bits with a sharp knife. Add all these trimmings to 8 cups (2 litres) of fish stock or water and add some carrot peelings, onion, celery scraps, and fresh thyme. Simmer 1 hour, then strain and use in a soup where required.

Smoked Salmon and Goat Cheese Terrine

Yield ❧ 8–10 appetizer servings or about 24 canapé size servings

This elegant appetizer can be made well ahead and served quickly. Care should be taken when you are cutting it. Make sure the terrine is very cold and the knife you are using is hot—immerse in very hot water and dry quickly between every cut when you are trimming into canapé-size portions. Cut into small squares, it is visually arresting and also crowd-pleasingly tasty.

8 oz (200 g) goat cheese
8 oz (200 g) unsalted butter
3 Tbsp (45 ml) fresh chives, chopped
1 shallot, finely chopped
salt and pepper, to taste
Tabasco, to taste
1 lb (450 g) smoked salmon, thinly sliced

pastry bag
small loaf pan

Warm the cheese and butter by leaving them on top of a warm oven for 30 minutes. When warmed and soft, place both in the bowl of an electric mixer with a paddle attachment and beat until light and fluffy, about 3 minutes. Add the chives, shallot, salt, pepper, and Tabasco and beat for 1 minute further to incorporate the seasonings. Remove to a pastry bag fitted with a medium straight (not fluted) tip.

Spray the loaf pan with cooking spray, or brush lightly with vegetable oil. Line the pan with plastic wrap, allowing excess to come out over the edge by 2 inches on every side. Line the bottom of the pan completely with a single layer of the smoked salmon, using ¼ of the salmon. Pipe ⅙ of the cheese mixture over the surface of the salmon and with a small palate knife or spatula, spread it out to cover the salmon completely. Add another layer of salmon and repeat the process 5 more times, finishing with a final layer of salmon. Bring the excess plastic wrap up and lay it over top of the mould. Press down firmly to compress the terrine a bit. Place the terrine in a refrigerator for at least 2–4 hours, but note that this may be prepared up to one week in advance. To portion, ensure that it is very cold and firm to the touch.

To serve: Remove the terrine by unfolding the plastic wrap from the top and carefully inverting the mould onto a cutting board. While pressing down on the unfolded plastic, gently pull up on the loaf pan to remove. Have a container of very hot water nearby and a long, thin, very sharp knife in the water, heating up the blade.

Remove the plastic wrap carefully from the terrine and, using the very hot knife, cut the terrine into slices. For canapé portions, cut each slice into bite-size pieces. They can be served on their own or on top of toasted pumpernickel.

Smoked Scallops with Jerusalem Artichoke Purée and Basil Oil

Yield ⌒ 6 servings

Smoked scallops are easy to prepare on a home barbecue or smoker. Smoke them over high heat so that they smoke and cook at the same time, then eat them right out of the smoker. If the scallops cool down and are reheated, they can become quite dry. The Jerusalem Artichoke Purée can be made vegan if desired by omitting the cream and butter and it is still surprisingly rich.

36 medium scallops

Jerusalem Artichoke Purée

1.10 lbs (500 g) large Jerusalem artichokes, carefully peeled and cut into ½-inch (1-cm) chunks

1 large onion, peeled and cut into 4 large wedges

1 small celeriac, peeled and cubed

6 cloves garlic

6 cups (1.5 litres) vegetable stock or water

¼ cup (50 ml) unsweetened heavy cream, whipped into soft peaks, optional

2 Tbsp (30 ml) butter, optional

salt and Tabasco, to taste

Basil Oil

1 bunch (about 500 ml) fresh basil leaves, washed, patted dry, and stems removed

a pinch of salt + salt, to taste

2 tsp (10 ml) Pernod, sambuca, or ouzo

1 ½ cups (300 ml) extra virgin olive oil

To prepare the Basil Oil, combine the basil leaves, pinch of salt, and Pernod, sambuca, or ouzo in a blender. With the blender running, gradually add the olive oil in a slow steady stream until it is incorporated and the purée is smooth. Continue to blend another minute—this will make it very lustrous. Remove the oil from the blender and place it in a clean empty squirt bottle.

To prepare the Jerusalem Artichoke Purée, place the Jerusalem artichokes, onions, celeriac, and garlic in a large pot and just cover them with the vegetable stock or water. Bring to a hard boil, reduce heat to medium-high, and cook for 30 minutes, or until the vegetables are thoroughly cooked and virtually mushy. Strain off the liquid and reserve it. Place the purée in a blender and blend until very smooth. If it is too stiff, add as much of the reserved cooking liquid as is necessary to create a very smooth purée, the texture of stiff pancake batter. Add the butter and the unsweetened cream if desired. Whisk in until it has dissolved. Add salt and Tabasco to taste.

To prepare the scallops: In a smoker, or on the barbecue, smoke the scallops over medium-high heat for about 20 minutes. They should be thoroughly cooked but not too dry.

To serve, place a pile of the artichoke purée in the middle of a serving plate, forming a circle. Place the hot scallops on top of the purée and surround them with the Basil Oil. Serve immediately.

Smoked Eel Ravioli with Saffron Cream

Yield ⌒ 6 servings

This recipe requires a little time and effort but makes a spectacular appetizer for a special dinner party.

Pasta

2 cups (400 ml) all-purpose flour
3 eggs
½ cup (125 ml) water
1 tsp (5 ml) salt

pasta roller

Filling

6 oz (170 g) smoked eel, skin and small bones
   removed, roughly chopped
4 oz (113 g) soft goat cheese or cream cheese
1 egg, beaten + 1 egg, beaten with 1 tsp (5 ml)
   water
1 tsp (5 ml) chopped chives or green onions
1 tsp (5 ml) chopped fresh sage
salt and pepper, to taste

Saffron Cream Sauce

1 cup (200 ml) white wine
1 shallot, minced
pinch of saffron, about 20 threads
pinch of turmeric
1 cup (200 ml) heavy whipping cream
1 tsp (5 ml) butter
salt to taste
Tabasco to taste
4 basil leaves, sliced
1 Tbsp (15 ml) lemon juice
4 cherry tomatoes, thinly sliced, for garnish

To prepare the pasta, place the flour, salt, and eggs in the bowl of a food processor. Process until the mixture resembles the texture of cornmeal. With the motor running, add just enough water to make the dough come together in a big ball. Remove the dough from the processor into a bowl, add a dash of flour, and knead for 1–2 minutes. Flatten the dough into a disc shape, wrap it in plastic wrap, and let chill up to 1 hour in the fridge.

To prepare the filling, mix all ingredients except the egg mixed with water in a bowl. Stir until they are combined thoroughly.

Using a pasta roller, roll out two long 40-inch (1-m) sheets of pasta. Start rolling at the thickest setting then gradually step down to the #5 setting on your roller, to get nice even sheets. Lay the sheets out on a well-floured countertop. Space out 24 equal amounts of filling (about 1 oz/30 g each) along one sheet. Using a pastry brush, brush the pasta between the filling with the beaten egg. Carefully lay the second sheet of pasta over top of the first and press down on the edges of each pile of filling to seal. With a pasta cutter or sharp knife, cut out the individual raviolis and remove them to a floured tray.

To make the sauce: Add the wine and shallot to a medium heavy-bottom saucepan and bring to a boil. Add the saffron and turmeric and reduce by half. Add the cream and reduce by half again. Add the lemon juice and stir to combine. Stir in the butter, salt, Tabasco and basil leaves. Reserve in a warm place.

Bring a large pot of salted water to boil, add the ravioli, and cook 2–3 minutes. To serve, place 4 ravioli on each plate. Top with sauce and garnish with sliced cherry tomatoes.

Sole

SOLE HAS BEEN THE CENTREPIECE OF CLASSIC French fish recipes such as Sole à la Meunière and Sole Almondine since Carême commanded the stoves at Versailles. To this day, these recipes are served around the globe by a wide variety of chefs as exemplars of French gastronomy, yet the dishes are very much open to interpretation.

As the flavour of sole is so delicate, it is usually served with a subtle and nuanced sauce rather than a very aggressive one.

Sole stuffed with Smoked Salmon Mousse

Yield ⌒ 4 servings

A great party dish to prepare ahead, leave on a tray in the oven, and cook for fifteen minutes whenever you are ready. If you have saved any salmon scraps or belly pieces from trimming the salmon filets earlier in this book, you may use them in this recipe. Dover sole, flounder, and haddock all make excellent substitutions to the grey sole. This dish is excellent with Shrimp Americaine Sauce (page 44).

SERVE WITH
white rice and steamed vegetables

7 oz (200 g) smoked salmon with noticeable
    smoke flavour

3.5 oz (100 g) salmon scraps, chopped

½ tsp (2 ml) salt

ground white pepper, to taste

1 shallot, peeled and cut into small chunks

1 small egg, lightly beaten

3 Tbsp (45 ml) heavy whipping cream, cold

1 Tbsp (15 ml) chives or green onions, thinly
    sliced

8 filets grey sole (2–3 oz/60–85 g each)

butter, for pan

1 cup (200 ml) fish stock or water

½ cup (100 ml) white wine

toothpicks

In the bowl of a food processor, add the smoked salmon, salmon scraps, salt, white pepper, and shallot. Purée for 1 minute. Add the egg and purée 1 additional minute. Add the cream in a slow steady stream until it is incorporated. Remove the seafood mousse from the bowl and place it in a clean container. Stir in the chives or green onions and place the mousse in the fridge for 20 minutes to firm up.

Preheat the oven to 350°F (180°C). Take each filet and place ⅛ of the fish purée on the filet near the tail end. Roll up the filet gently, taking care not to squeeze out any mousse. Secure the roll with a toothpick.

Butter a high-sided sheet pan or baking dish. Pour the fish stock and wine into the pan. Place the 8 stuffed filets in the pan with the filling sides facing up. Bake in the oven for 15 minutes or until mousse is just set and fish flakes easily.

Sole Poached in Apple Cider

Yield ☙ 6 servings

This is a regional interpretation of the traditional poached Dover Sole with Verjus Sauce. I have replaced the verjus with local apple cider and a little wine for piquancy. If you don't have sole, you can try using haddock, plaice, or hake.

12 sole filets (1–2 oz/50 g each)
4 cups (1 litre) + ½ cup (100 ml) apple cider
6 sprigs fresh thyme
3 bay leaves
1 tsp (5 ml) peppercorns
1 cup (200 ml) white wine
1 small onion, peeled and sliced
1 Tbsp (15 ml) cornstarch

butcher's twine

Roll each of the filets into a cylinder shape and tie with butcher's twine.

In a large pot bring the 4 cups (1 litre) of cider, thyme, bay leaves, peppercorns, wine, and onion to a simmer over medium heat. When the liquid is simmering, adjust the heat to medium-low and carefully add the tied fish bundles. Poach the fish in this liquid for 6–8 minutes, gently turning the bundles with a slotted spoon to ensure even cooking.

After the filets are cooked, remove them to a tray and carefully cut the strings with scissors. Reserve in a warm place.

Prepare a slurry by combining the ½ cup (100 ml) of apple cider and cornstarch. Add the slurry to the cooking liquid and increase heat to high. When the liquid reaches a boil it should thicken a little. Strain through a fine sieve. Place 3 cooked filets on each plate and top with sauce.

Squid

SQUID IS PREVALENT IN MANY CULTURES. From Greece to Thailand, from the smallest calamari to the largest cuttlefish, the trick is to either cook it minimally or to tenderize it by cooking it for a long time.

Flash-Grilled Calamari

Yield ❧ 6–8 servings

This is quick and easy if you have cleaned the squid ahead of time. Cooked quickly on a really hot patio grill in the summer, served over an arugula or mesclun green salad, this is an excellent starter. You're going to be using the bottom of heavy flat bottomed frying pan in this recipe, so make sure that the bottom of it is very clean. The frying pan or pot is used to weigh down the calamari while it is being grilled so that it stays flat on the grill.

2 ¼ lbs (1 kg) squid, cleaned, bodies left whole
¼ cup (60 ml) + 1 Tbsp (15 ml) extra virgin
    olive oil
salt and pepper, to taste
cayenne pepper, to taste
2 sprigs fresh rosemary
2 cloves garlic, sliced
1 tsp (5 ml) balsamic vinegar
fresh baby arugula or mesclun greens
    (or any young green salad)
1 tsp (5 ml) fresh lemon juice

cooking spray
large, heavy, flat-bottomed frying pan

Leaving the bodies whole, mix the squid with the ¼ cup (50 ml) of olive oil, salt, black pepper, cayenne pepper, rosemary (sprigs left whole), and garlic. Marinate until ready to grill; about 1 hour is best.

Preheat the grill on high until it is almost smoking. Drain the calamari from the marinade, reserving the rosemary. Spray the hot grill and the bottom of a clean, heavy frying pan or pot with some non-stick cooking spray. Watch out for the inevitable flare up, but you want it hot!

Carefully, but quickly, throw the rosemary sprigs into the flames. Place the calamari bodies and tentacles on the grill surface with the heavy pan on top to keep the squid flat. Turn the heat down to medium and cook for 2 minutes. Remove the pan, flip the squid with tongs, and replace the pan. Cook for another 1–2 minutes or until the squid is cooked through. With tongs, remove the squid from the grill. There should be some pleasing grill marks and smoky bits from the burning rosemary—this is desirable.

In a large bowl, toss the greens with the 1 Tbsp (15 ml) olive oil and the balsamic vinegar and place them on a serving plate. In the same bowl, add the still-hot squid and lemon juice and toss to coat. Place squid on top of the greens and drizzle a little more olive oil on top. Serve immediately.

Squid Stuffed with Ricotta and Spinach

Yield ⌒ 8 servings

This Italian-inspired recipe makes a great appetizer in the summertime or for an Italian-themed dinner party. Do not overstuff the calamari bodies or they could burst. Add the stuffing until the squid are three-quarters full, then secure.

SERVE WITH
Soave, Greco di Tufo, or Roero Arneis wine from Italy and polenta with parmigiano reggiano cheese

16 medium squid (2.2 lbs/1 kg total)
1 medium onion, minced
1 garlic clove, minced
1 Tbsp (15 ml) + 1 Tbsp (15 ml) extra virgin olive oil
1 Tbsp (15 ml) unsalted butter
½ lb (200 g) fresh spinach, trimmed of any stems, rinsed, and chopped
1 ½ cups (300 g) ricotta cheese
1 egg
1 Tbsp (15 ml) finely chopped Italian parsley
1 tsp (5 ml) coarse salt
fresh ground pepper, to taste
½ tsp (2 ml) red chile flakes
½ cup (100 ml) dry white wine
1 (13 oz/400 ml) can of Italian tomatoes, roughly chopped
2 cloves garlic, sliced
2 lemons, quartered

Preheat the oven to 375°F (190°C). Clean the squid and chop the tentacles finely. Set them aside. Over medium heat, sauté the onion and garlic in 1 Tbsp (15 ml) of the olive oil and the butter until the onions are soft, about 4 minutes.

Add the tentacles and cook for 2 minutes. Add the spinach and sauté, stirring, until it has wilted. Drain off any extra liquid and cool the spinach mixture.

In a mixing bowl, combine the ricotta, egg, parsley, and cooled spinach mixture. Mix thoroughly and season with the salt, pepper, and chile flakes.

Loosely stuff the mixture into the squid bodies and close the openings securely with toothpicks.

Use the remaining 1 Tbsp (15 ml) of olive oil to grease a rectangular baking dish large enough to hold the squid comfortably in one layer.

Arrange the squid in the dish and add the wine, tomatoes, and garlic. Season with salt, pepper, and more chile flakes if you wish.

Bake for 40–45 minutes, or until the squid is tender and the sauce has thickened. If there is too much sauce, raise the oven temperature and allow the liquid to reduce. If there is too little, add more white wine. Serve the squid with the lemon quarters.

Crispy Calamari

Yield ℘ 4-6 servings

What is the trick to cooking calamari properly so that it is tender inside but crunchy on the outside? At our restaurant we eschew a thick batter and go for a simple dredging in a special flour mixture. Our secret? Graham cracker crumbs mixed with flour.

SERVE WITH
wedges of lemon and Smoked Tomato Sauce
(page 54)

1.10 lbs (500 g) fresh squid
1 cup (200 ml) all-purpose flour
1 cup (200 ml) unsweetened graham cracker
  crumbs
1 tsp (5 ml) salt
1 tsp (5 ml) ground black pepper

**countertop fryer or large pot of oil heated to
  375°F (190°C)**

Clean the calamari and carefully peel off any skin with your fingers; it should come off relatively easily. Pull the tentacles out of the bodies.

Cut the tentacles just above the eyes and beak and reserve. Carefully reach inside the cavity of the squid and feel for the clear quill. It will pull out easily. Squeeze any excess mass out of the body. Keep the tentacles whole and cut the body into ¼-inch (½-cm) rings. Pat dry with paper towels.

In a large bowl, mix the flour, graham cracker crumbs, salt, and pepper. Add the cleaned, chopped calamari body and tentacles and dredge thoroughly. Shake off excess crumbs and place the calamari in the fryer. If you do not have a large fryer, make 2 or 3 batches—do not overcrowd the oil or the temperature will drop too much. Fry briskly for 2 minutes or until the outsides are crunchy. Do not overcook.

Remove the calamari from the oil and place them in a bowl that has been lined liberally with paper towel to absorb excess oil. Sprinkle salt on the calamari while they are still hot. Repeat with the remaining squid.

Sturgeon

STURGEON ONCE TEEMED IN THE COASTAL waterways of Atlantic Canada and northern New England, and they were particularly plentiful in the Bay of Fundy and St. John River. Sturgeon's robust texture and unique flavour made it a staple among the area's indigenous peoples.

In the 1700s sturgeon caviar became one of the most sought-after delicacies at the table of the cosmopolitan courts of St. Petersburg, Moscow, and eventually Paris and London. Demand soared worldwide and caviar-dispensing dynasties like Petrossian rose to prominence, wealth, and power. Alas, the once-plentiful sturgeon has been hunted virtually out of existence because of demand for its roe. Caviar now costs upwards of two-hundred dollars per ounce due to its scarcity.

Luckily, there are an ever-increasing number of land-based sturgeon farms worldwide that are helping to repopulate depleted stocks. I have a favourite supplier in Blacks Harbour, New Brunswick (Supreme Sturgeon and Caviar), which is raising short-nosed sturgeon from wild fish originally caught in the Bay of Fundy. My friend Don Breau is raising them as well, for the caviar trade, but what to do with the male fish? Well, we can benefit from this and enjoy sturgeon in a variety of different ways.

New Brunswick Sturgeon with a Crunchy Falafel Crust, Orange Gastrique, and Black Olive Oil

Yield ↝ 4 servings

This is a showpiece recipe for when the boss is over or you are out to impress your significant other or foodie dinner guest. You can do a little advance work by making the orange sauce and black olive oil ahead, crusting the fish and searing it. All you need to do then is pop the fish in the oven for 10–12 minutes and serve.

Hake, sablefish, black cod, or salmon will also work in place of the sturgeon. Falafel mix can be found in most bulk food stores, but it may be best to pick it up at a Middle Eastern deli, where you can also find the cured black olives.

SERVE WITH
a ragout of roasted vegetables with a hint of curry or fresh herbs and a fruity red wine like Beaujolais

Orange Gastrique
½ cup (100 ml) orange juice
¼ cup (50 ml) white wine
1 tsp (5 ml) white wine vinegar
salt and Tabasco, to taste
2 cloves garlic, minced
2 shallots, minced
½ cup (100 ml) sugar

Black Olive Oil
1 cup (100 g) cured black olives, pitted
¾ cup (150 ml) extra virgin olive oil

Falafel-Encrusted Sturgeon
½ cup (100 ml) ready-made falafel mix
4 portions sturgeon filet (5 oz/150 g each)
2 Tbsp (30 ml) extra virgin olive oil or grapeseed oil

To make the black olive oil, place the pitted olives and the ¾ cup (150 ml) olive oil in a blender. Purée at high speed until smooth. Remove to a small bowl and reserve.

Clean the blender, then make the Orange Gastrique. Place the orange juice, wine, vinegar, salt, Tabasco, garlic, and shallots in the blender. Blend until smooth, about 1 minute. Pour the mixture into a small saucepan and add the sugar. Bring to a boil, reduce the heat to medium, and cook for 5–7 minutes, or until reduced by half and thickened. Remove the sauce from heat and let it cool to room temperature. If, when cool, the liquid is a little too thick to pour, whisk in a couple drops of warm water or orange juice. Reserve.

Preheat the oven to 400°F (200°C).

Place the falafel mix in a pie pan and coat and dredge the sturgeon filets carefully on both sides. Pat down to encourage adherence of the mix.

Heat a non-stick frying pan over medium heat and add the olive or grapeseed oil. Fry the filets in the oil until the crust is crispy, about 3 minutes.

Flip filets over and repeat on other side. Remove to a sheet tray, place in the oven, and bake 10 minutes or until the fish is cooked through. Place each piece of fish in the middle of a plate and surround with a drizzle of the Gastrique and Black Olive Oil.

Swordfish

MANY PEOPLE (INCLUDING ME) HAVE READ the book *The Perfect Storm*, or watched the movie adaptation with George Clooney. The conditions that sword fishers have had to endure in search of the mighty billed fish are gut-wrenching.

Second only to tuna as a valued catch, swordfish's dense, rich flesh holds up well on long fishing trips when iced in the hold of a ship awaiting return to port. But swordfish are only caught far out to sea, so the massive effort put into catching them is, in a way, Herculean.

Swordfish is well-suited to many cooking techniques, is meaty and tasty, and can hold up to marinades, crusts, hearty sauces, and relishes.

Roast Swordfish with Tequila-Lime Sauce and Spicy Mexican Rice

Yield ☙ 6 servings

I trained as a chef in Chicago and apprenticed at Everest, a well-known French restaurant there. At the time, I did not know about the massive Latino (and especially Mexican) population of the third-largest city in the U.S.

At Everest, there were seventeen kitchen employees working on any given Saturday night, and fifteen of them were from the Oaxaca province of Mexico. They were great cooks, hard workers, and loyal to their families and friends. Every day at 4:00 PM, just before service began, the entire restaurant staff would sit together for half an hour and have a communal meal, "La Comida," prepared by the cooks. Quite often this would be traditional Mexican peasant food, which I enjoyed immensely. The rice accompanying this recipe was one of my favourites from their repertoire. Halibut and tuna work in place of the swordfish.

6 swordfish filets or steaks (4–5 oz /150 g each)
salt and pepper, to taste
1 Tbsp (15 ml) extra virgin olive oil

Tequila Lime Sauce
4 Tbsp (60 ml) tequila
½ cup (100 ml) corn syrup
1 clove garlic, minced
½ inch (1 cm) fresh ginger, peeled and minced
½ tsp (2 ml) salt
fresh ground black pepper, to taste
juice and zest from 2 large limes★
1 Tbsp (15 ml) butter, optional

★Soak the limes in warm water for 20
  minutes before zesting and juicing

Spicy Mexican Rice
1 cup (200 ml) water
1 cup (200 ml) tomato juice
½ cup (100 ml) salsa + salsa, to taste
1 jalapeno, seeded and chopped
1 Tbsp (15 ml) lemon juice
1 tsp (5 ml) salt
1 small onion, peeled and roughly chopped
6 sprigs fresh cilantro, stems and all + cilantro,
  to taste
2 cups (400 ml) parboiled rice

To make the sauce, combine the tequila, corn syrup, garlic, ginger, salt, pepper, lime zest and juice in a sauce pot and bring to a simmer over medium heat. (The alcohol in the tequila will evaporate by boiling but if you have a gas range watch out for a flare-up.) Simmer for 5 minutes then turn off the heat. Whisk in the butter, if desired. Keep the sauce warm and reserve.

To prepare the rice, combine the water, tomato juice, ½ cup (100 ml) salsa, jalapeno, lemon juice, salt, onion, and 6 sprigs cilantro in a blender. Blend until smooth.

Combine the rice and puréed liquid and cook the rice according to package directions. (Approximately 18 minutes on a stovetop). While a rice cooker is preferable, rice cooked with the stovetop method will work as well. When the rice is cooked, fluff with a fork and stir in extra salsa and cilantro, if desired.

Season the fish with the salt, pepper, and olive oil. Grill on a preheated grill for 4–5 minutes each side, or until cooked to your liking.

Place the finished fish on the rice. Top with sauce and serve. Garnish with fresh cilantro.

ETHICAL EATING NOTE

Alas, swordfish's popularity has meant inevitable overfishing, especially by unsustainable methods that include longlining. Some conscientious governments have actually made significant regulatory decisions to limit swordfish quotas, and for a number of years, many influential North American chefs have honoured a voluntary moratorium on purchasing and serving swordfish. This has resulted in a minor resurgence in the populations, but not to the degree that can justify longlining. Please ask your fishmonger for harpooned Atlantic swordfish (this is considered a sustainable method of harvesting), and scold them if they are buying from longliners.

Pan-Roasted Swordfish with Pesto-Tomato Relish

Yield ⤳ 6 servings

This is an Italian idea that I learned in a French restaurant in an American city, and now I cook it at a small Canadian restaurant—this is the epitome of global cuisine. Ripe tomatoes, especially in season, multicolored if available, are combined in a pesto and balsamic dressing with capers and served as a room temperature relish over pan-roasted swordfish. The fish would also be delicious cooked on a grill.

SERVE WITH
mashed potatoes

1 Pesto recipe (see below)

4 ripe tomatoes, 2 red and 2 yellow, or 24 grape or cherry tomatoes (multi-coloured if available)

1 Tbsp (15 ml) capers

1 Tbsp (15 ml) balsamic vinegar

¼ cup (50 ml) extra virgin olive oil

salt and pepper, to taste

6 swordfish filets or steaks (5.29 oz/150 g each), about ¾-inch (2 cm) thick

salt, pepper, and olive oil, to taste

olive oil, grapeseed oil, or butter, for sautéing

Pesto

1 ½ cups (300 ml) fresh basil leaves

½ cup (100 ml) pine nuts, toasted

3 cloves garlic, minced

salt and pepper, to taste

½ cup (100 ml) extra virgin olive oil

½ cup (100 ml) grated parmigiano reggiano cheese

Make the pesto by placing the basil, pine nuts, garlic, salt, and pepper in the bowl of a food processor and puréeing for 1 minute while gradually adding the ½ cup olive oil. Add the cheese and pulse it in briefly. Remove to a small bowl and refrigerate for 1 hour or more to let the flavours set.

If using large red and yellow tomatoes, cut a shallow X on the bottom of each tomato with a sharp paring knife. Drop the tomatoes in some rapidly boiling water for 10 seconds or so. Immediately place them in ice water to stop the cooking. With a paring knife, peel away the skin of the tomatoes. Cut the tomatoes in half and gently remove the seeds. Carefully cut into ½-inch (1-cm) cubes. (If using grape or cherry tomatoes, simply quarter them.)

Place the tomatoes, capers, and balsamic vinegar in the pesto mixture, thin with the ¼ cup (50 ml) olive oil, and season with salt and pepper. Add more balsamic vinegar if you prefer a more acidic flavour.

Season the fish with salt and pepper and a little good olive oil.

In a heavy or cast iron frying pan that has been heated over medium-high heat, sear the fish in a little olive oil, grapeseed oil, or butter until golden brown on one side, 3 minutes or so. Carefully flip over and repeat on the other side. Place the pan in a hot oven for an additional 3–4 minutes.

Place each fish on a plate, slicing it into bite-size portions if desired. Top with the Pesto Tomato Relish.

Swordfish Kebabs on Orange and Date Couscous

Yield ⌒ 6–8 servings

These kebabs are great fun for the adventurous family to make and enjoy outdoors. Use whatever fruit and vegetables suit your fancy; the ones included are an example but any fruit is great on the grill, especially when paired with fish. Both the ground sumac and the mulberry syrup can be found at Middle Eastern markets.

Swordfish Kebabs

1 tsp (5 ml) ground coriander

1 tsp (5 ml) ground sumac

1 Tbsp (15 ml) mulberry syrup, optional

1 Tbsp (15 ml) fresh lemon juice

½ cup (100 ml) fresh mint leaves, chopped roughly

2 Tbsp (30 ml) extra virgin olive oil

2 ¼ lbs (1 kg) swordfish, cut into ½-inch (2-cm) cubes

1 small green zucchini, cut into ½-inch (2-cm) cubes

1 large ripe mango, or fruit of your choice, cut into ½-inch (2-cm) cubes

18 large cherry tomatoes

12–14 mushrooms

salt and pepper, to taste

12–14 (11-inch/30-cm) skewers, soaked 2 hours in water if wooden

Couscous

¾ cup (150 ml) water or vegetable stock

¾ cup (150 ml) orange juice

1 ½ cups (300 ml) instant couscous

12 fresh dates, pitted and chopped

2 Tbsp (30 ml) Italian parsley, stemmed and chopped

1 Tbsp (15 ml) butter

salt and pepper, to taste

Combine the coriander, sumac, mulberry syrup, lemon juice, mint, and olive oil in a glass container large enough to hold the fish. Marinate the fish in the liquid for up to 2 hours—no more or the lemon juice will seviche the fish.

Skewer the fish, vegetables, and fruit, alternating between them so that each skewer has a variety. Retain any leftover marinade. Season with salt and pepper, and reserve.

To make the couscous, combine the water or stock and orange juice in a saucepan that has a tight-fitting lid. Bring to a boil, then add the couscous. Stir briefly, replace the lid, and turn the heat off. Steam the couscous 10 minutes. After 10 minutes, remove the cover and fluff the couscous with a fork. Add the dates, parsley, butter, salt, and pepper, and replace the lid. Allow to steam an additional 5 minutes.

To cook the kebabs, preheat the grill. Spray the cooking surface with cooking spray, then put the kebabs on the grill. Brush the kebabs with the remaining marinade, then continue cooking for 3 minutes per side, or until the fish is cooked but the tomatoes are not mushy.

Serve immediately on a bed of couscous.

Tuna

THE FOODIE'S PERENNIAL FAVOURITE, TUNA was long thought by most of North American society to be found only in a small can in the supermarket aisles. Fresh tuna in North America was unheard of.

With France's nouvelle cuisine movement, tuna suddenly became massively popular. Seared on the outside but still raw (like sushi) in the middle, this method of preparing tuna captured the best of east and west in current culinary trends. To this day, tuna reigns supreme on many menus as the pre-eminent luxury dish of great restaurants.

Black and White Sesame–Crusted Tuna with Miso Broth and Noodles

Yield ✑ 4 servings

This is a cross between a Japanese miso soup and a hearty Vietnamese pho and makes a great main course dish. You can find most of the ingredients below at an Asian market.

SERVE WITH
sake or a German Riesling

1.32 lbs (600 g) tuna loin, cut into 4 portions
salt and pepper, to taste
1 Tbsp (15 ml) sesame oil
4 cups (1 litre) water or vegetable stock
½ cup (100 ml) miso paste
2 Tbsp (30 ml) tamari or good quality soy
    sauce
1 tsp (5 ml) sambal olek (garlic chile sauce)
1 red onion thinly sliced
½ a carrot, sliced thinly and julienned
 5 oz (100 g) soba, yuba or other thin noodles,
    cooked
¼ cup (50 g) white sesame seeds
¼ cup (50 g) black sesame seeds
2 Tbsp (30 ml) vegetable or canola oil
edible seaweed like wakame or hijiki, soaked in
    warm water for 30 minutes, optional
enoki or other mushrooms, for garnish

Rub the tuna with the salt, pepper, and sesame oil and refrigerate while you make the broth.

Combine the water or vegetable stock, miso, tamari or soy sauce, sambal olek, onion, and carrot in a large pot. Bring to a boil and simmer 5 minutes. Add the noodles, return just to a simmer, and immediately turn off the heat while you finish the tuna.

In a small pie dish, combine the black and white sesame seeds and coat each side of the tuna portions by pressing the pieces firmly into the seed mixture. Heat a large skillet over medium heat and add the vegetable or canola oil. Cook the tuna in the oil for 2–3 minutes per side, or until the seed crust is crunchy and golden brown.

Remove the noodles from the broth with tongs and distribute them among 4 large bowls. Place a portion of tuna on top of each bowl of noodles and pour the remaining broth around it. Garnish with seaweed and enoki mushrooms and serve.

Seared Tuna with Saffron, Tomato, and Olive Oil Ragout

Yield ☙ 6 servings

Another longtime favourite at our restaurant. You can make the Saffron, Tomato, and Olive Oil Ragout (page 13) well ahead and simply reheat it and the tuna. We serve this atop really garlicky mashed potatoes or a white bean purée

2 lbs (900 g) centre-cut tuna loin, cut in 6
   portions, about ¾-inch (2-cm) thick
salt and pepper, to taste
1 ½ cups (300 ml) + 2 Tbsp (30 ml) olive oil
1 recipe Saffron, Tomato, and Olive Oil Ragout
   (page 13)
6 fresh basil leaves, thinly sliced

Rub the tuna loin pieces with 1 Tbsp (15 ml) of the olive oil and season them with salt and pepper. Marinate for 1 hour.

In a heavy cast iron pan over high heat, sear the tuna until it is browned and almost crispy on one side, about 2 minutes. Flip over and repeat on the other side. Remove from heat. Do not overcook.

Cut each tuna portion in half, exposing the rare centre and crispy crust. Arrange the pieces in the middle of a plate. Alternatively, cut the tuna into slices and fan them on a plate. Add the basil to the ragout, reheat briefly, then drizzle the sauce over the fish and around the plate. Serve immediately.

Tropical Tuna Tartare

Yield ∾ 6 servings (or 18 canapé servings)

This is a great recipe for getting your guests to eat sushi and sashimi painlessly. A tiny bit on a rice cracker or cucumber round makes a nice canapé, or a larger amount moulded in a ring mould with some nice greens makes an attractive and delicious first course.

SERVE WITH
organic sake

1.10 lbs (500 g) fresh yellowfin or albacore
    tuna loin
4 green onions, very thinly sliced
10 cilantro leaves, thinly sliced
1 tsp (5 ml) fresh ginger, finely minced
1 tsp (5 ml) fresh garlic, finely minced
1 Tbsp (15 ml) sesame seed oil
1 Tbsp (15 ml) tamari or other soy sauce
1 small tomato, peeled, seeded, and diced
2 Tbsp (30 ml) fresh mango, finely diced
1 tsp (5 ml) rice wine vinegar
salt and pepper, to taste
1 Tbsp (15 ml) black sesame seeds
2 Tbsp (30 ml) sushi ginger, julienned, for
    garnish

With a very sharp knife, cut the tuna carefully into very small (⅙-inch/5-mm or smaller) cubes. Combine the tuna with the remaining ingredients, except the sushi ginger and sesame seeds, and let the flavours meld for 10 minutes.

With a 1 ½-inch (4-cm) ring mould, or small tin with the top and bottom removed, place ⅙ of the fish mixture carefully on a serving plate. Top with a sprinkle of the black sesame seeds and remove the ring mould. Sprinkle some of the sushi ginger, cilantro leaves, and green onions on the tartare and around the plate as desired. Serve.

ETHICAL EATING NOTE

Tuna is the most valuable creature in the seas to the commercial fisher, mostly due to the demand of the Japanese sushi market. Indeed, some large grade-A bluefin tuna can be worth upwards of $35,000 (or more) per fish to a willing Japanese buyer! Because of this demand, tuna is a widely hunted species, and as a result the population is being decimated. The mighty bluefin is the biggest prize and in the most grave danger, but the Pacific yellowfin is at risk too.

I would encourage you to shop for harpooned or pole-and-troll tuna and opt for Atlantic yellowfin or albacore species, which are not as attractively deep red as bluefin, but are delicious and sustainable at present.

Recommended Suppliers

Acadian Sturgeon and Caviar
30 Carters Wharf Road
Carters Point, NB E5S 1S5
Phone: (506) 642-1816
Website: acadian-sturgeon.com

Afishionado Fishmongers
The Warehouse Market
2867 Isleville St.
Halifax, NS B3K 3X4

– or –

Afishionado Headquarters
10-275 Rocky Lake Dr.
Bedford, NS B4A 2T3
(902) 403-1178
Website: afishionado.ca

Birch Street Seafoods
35 Birch Street
Digby, NS B0V 1A0
(902) 245-6551
Website: facebook.com/BirchStreetSeafoods

Fisherman's Market
607 Bedford Hwy
Halifax, NS B3M 2L6
Phone (retail): 902-443-3474
Phone (wholesale): 902-445-3474
Fax: 902-443-5561
Website: fishermansmarket.ca

Hooked Inc.
Various locations in Toronto, ON
Website: hookedinc.ca

Innovative Fishery Products Inc.
3569 Hwy #1, PO Box 125
Belliveau Cove, NS B0W 1J0
Phone: 902-837-5163
Fax: 902-837-5165
Email: office@innovativefishery.com

Sober Island Oysters
104 Mozier Cove Road
Sheet Harbour, NS B0J 3B0
(902) 885-3040
Website: sober-island-oysters-ltd.business.site

Sustainable Blue
259 Red Bank Road
Centre Burlington, NS B0N 1E0
Website: sustainableblue.com